OPERATION
Julie

And then there came the night of the greatest ever raid
They arrested every drug that had ever been made
They took eighty-two laws
Through eighty-two doors
And they didn't halt the pull
Till the cells were all full
'Cos Julie was working for the Drug Squad

The Clash
(Strummer/Jones)

OPERATION Julie

The World's Greatest LSD Bust

Lyn Ebenezer

First impression: 2010
Third impression: 2015

© Lyn Ebenezer & Y Lolfa Cyf., 2010

Cover design: Y Lolfa

The publishers wish to thank Raymond Daniel,
Elizabeth Jones & Arvid Parry-Jones
for the use of the photographs.

ISBN: 978 184771 146 5

Printed on acid-free and partly recycled paper
and published and bound in Wales by
Y Lolfa Cyf., Talybont, Ceredigion SY24 5HE
e-mail ylolfa@ylolfa.com
website www.ylolfa.com
tel 01970 832 304
fax 832 782

INTRODUCTION

IN MARCH 1977 I was employed as a journalist by North Wales Newspapers in the Aberystwyth area. I was also fortunate to be able to add to my meagre wage by doing a considerable amount of freelance work for the *Western Mail* and BBC Radio. The emergence of the Free Wales Army in 1963 and their threat to the planned investiture of Prince Charles as Prince of Wales in 1969 had attracted much media attention, and I was often contacted by journalists working mainly out of Manchester.

Prior to the investiture, the prince spent a term at the University of Wales, Aberystwyth and, expecting trouble, the world's press descended on the town. As one of the few Welsh speakers among the press gang, I was regularly asked for assistance. These were days of pink champagne for breakfast and all-night drinking sessions. As a result, I managed to build up a considerable list of contacts among journalists working for the national dailies and Sundays.

It was one of these contacts, Jim Price of the *Daily Express*, that involuntarily led me to the heart of Operation Julie – at the time the biggest drugs bust in history. Jim, who lived in Deganwy, North Wales, had heard of arrests in Ceredigion and asked me to make inquiries on his behalf. It turned out to be a massive story.

As a result of the operation, members of LSD

manufacturing and marketing rings in London and mid Wales, responsible for producing some 60 million tabs selling for around £1 each on the street, were jailed for a total of 170 years. Those arrested were said to have been responsible for 90 per cent of the LSD produced in Britain and 60 per cent worldwide. That is the official line. It will become evident, however, that truth and fiction are still inextricably mixed over 30 years later. But the facts, incredible as they are, seem to outweigh the fiction. Here I include both.

London or another big city would have been a natural choice for such a huge manufacturing and marketing venture. But to locate an acid ring manufacturing and marketing the purest LSD in history in rural mid Wales, remote from ports and airports, would seem to be beyond the realms of fantasy. It may be that the remoteness of the Welsh production and distribution centres was actually the LSD empire's strength. Its main artery was the M4, leading from just south of Carmarthen through the Thames Valley into the heart of London. Just off the motorway, in copses and in stone walls, they organised pre-arranged dead letter drops where LSD was exchanged for cash.

The story of Operation Julie is, if you believe the official spin, the story of an ideal that went wrong, greed and audacious enterprise on one side and of diligent, selfless and determined police work on the other. But it is also a story of political infighting and lasting bitterness. Stories abound of undiscovered stashes of LSD and hidden fortunes. There are tales of tip-offs by disgruntled police officers and even a royal connection.

Despite its apparent success, all hopes among some of the officers of forming a national drugs squad were dashed. Under no circumstances were the officers to even extend the investigation beyond the remit of concentrating on those in custody as a result of Operation Julie arrests. So, within months of the termination of the investigation no less that six key officers, including the man who masterminded the operation, left the force in utter disillusion and bitterness.

There remain many unanswered questions. There are, for instance, accusations that statistics were deliberately massaged in order to strengthen the case for a national drugs squad. And if chemist Richard Kemp had produced LSD worth £2.5 million during his seven years of production, as was alleged, why was it that only £11,000 of his money was ever discovered?

Were the dangers of LSD exaggerated? Much was made of Kemp's ability to produce the purest LSD in history. Surely, if it was the purest, was it not also the safest? After all, the dangers of LSD lie in its impurities. In fact, despite lurid newspaper accounts of the dangers of acid, no evidence whatever was produced to prove that Kemp's LSD caused any deaths.

There are accusations that some officers, the operation's commander Dick Lee in particular, leaked doctored information to the press, especially to the red tops, as a means of strengthening the case for the formation of a national drugs squad. Papers like the *Daily Mirror* and the *Daily Express* in particular, following the sentencing, were laughably sensational. It is no coincidence that the only two books immediately published on Operation Julie appeared with the cooperation of those very newspapers. Dick Lee's book *Operation Julie* (W H Allen, 1978) was co-written by Colin Pratt of the *Express* while *Busted* by Martyn Pritchard and Ed Laxton (1978), riddled with police and underworld parlance, was published by Mirror Books. Was it a coincidence that the journalist who first alerted me to the swoop was a *Daily Express* reporter?

For those parts of the story detailing the mechanics of the operation itself, I have depended heavily on Dick Lee's book (long out of print). I have also been greatly helped by Martyn Pritchard's account and Stewart Tendler and David May's *The Brotherhood of Eternal Love* (1984). David Black's *Acid: The Secret History of LSD* (Vision Paperbacks, 1998) offers a fascinating insight to the international aspect of the LSD trade and the involvement of intelligence agencies and even governments on both side of the Atlantic. Andy Roberts' recently published book *Albion Dreaming: A Popular History of LSD in Britain* was invaluable.

I have included a chapter on a fascinating character who appeared in Llanddewi Brefi seemingly out of nowhere at the end of the sixties. David Litvinoff was not directly involved with the Julie story, but was very much a part of the drugs scene. He attracted many pop stars including the Stones, Eric Clapton, Jimi Hendrix and possibly Bob Dylan to his house. Albeit unaware of the fact, he was the harbinger of the influx of free spirits to the area.

Despite the trumpeted success of Operation Julie, the LSD market was merely temporarily dented. By the time the main perpetrators were jailed, LSD was again cheaply and easily obtainable. Pritchard claims it reached £8 a dose as a result of Operation Julie's success. Before long, however, the price had dropped to its previous level.

My motive in writing this book is not to be judgemental. Largely it is, rather, a story of how a quiet area of mid Wales was changed completely by incomers that embraced a different culture and way of life. Yet many of those involved in the LSD conspiracy were accepted by the local community. Had they not been embraced – or at least tolerated – their illegal venture would never have lasted so long. It is still difficult to find anyone in the Tregaron and Llanddewi Brefi area that will condemn them. In fact, they are regarded as likeable rouges, much like the area's own Robin Hood, the sixteenth-century robber and folk-hero Twm Shôn Cati.

So, even though this book follows the main events of Operation Julie, it is a revised overview. It is also the story of rural communities that were changed completely, and remain completely changed. LSD may not have changed the world, as its proponents had hoped it would, but it did, albeit inadvertently, change forever a rural way of life.

Lyn Ebenezer
Spring 2010

1

COUNTRY ROADS

THERE IS AN APOCRYPHAL story of Prince Charles, just before his investiture in 1969, being introduced to a hill farmer near Tregaron in the heart of rural Ceredigion. Observing the sparse landscape of reeds, gorse, stunted trees and peaty land, he inquired of the old man: 'What in the world can one produce in this sort of place?' The old character answered simply in two words: 'Men, Sir.' He could well have added: 'And LSD.'

Blaencaron is such an area. It is one of a number of small valleys spreading like veins into the heart of the market town of Tregaron in mid Wales, but runs out of road some three miles into the hills. Through it runs a brook, Nant Croes, giving the valley its alternative name, Cwm Croes (Traverse Vale). For centuries it was home to small farmers and crofters who scratched and eked a living out of the sparse and stony hillside fields. They were simple, God-fearing people; the sturdy, hardy country folk portrayed in R S Thomas' poems and in Kyffin Williams' landscape paintings. They stubbornly clung to their livelihoods like limpets clinging to rocks, defying the threatening tides of change.

The heart of the valley's social life was Blaencaron

Chapel, opened in 1876 and doubling as a schoolhouse and social centre that also catered for people's needs for entertainment. That entertainment meant, in the main, competitive concerts. There would be singing and reciting, reading unpunctuated passages and composing simple rhymes. There was even a choir. They made their own entertainment. Their radios were turned on mostly for weather forecasts and were always silenced on the seventh day, save for the Sunday morning service. English was a foreign language.

During the Second World War it was in an upstairs room of the Chapel House that locals congregated in a protest meeting against the War Office's threat to confiscate land, as it had done on Epynt Mountain in Breconshire and at Trawsfynydd in Gwynedd. The locals were assured that the take-over would only be temporary. But they knew from what had happened in other places that any change would be permanent.

Present at that meeting was Miss Cassie Davies, a future HM Schools' Inspector and staunch patriot. She sat among farmers who had previously been docile and compliant, but had been transformed into angry protesters who swore to defend their land and their livelihood to the death.

Cassie Davies, a stubborn and doughty Margaret Rutherford look-alike, years later described her feelings in her autobiography, *Hwb i'r Galon* (A Fillip to the Heart): 'There was never a meeting to compare with this in my lifetime. To witness and hear the quiet farmers of the locality awakening to the value of the land and the traditions and way of life... I swallowed many tears at that meeting. That is when I first experienced the grasp of the land.'

Even as late as the sixties of the last century, Blaencaron would be regarded as the archetypal area for anyone wanting to witness an example of a typical Welsh-speaking enclave. This was the era of the last of the monoglot Welsh speakers. But the land was gradually loosening its hold and change would be both sudden and overwhelming.

Crofters were getting old. Family succession, the bedrock of small farming communities, was rapidly losing its appeal. Children who once would have left school at fifteen to toil on their parents' farm were urged to further their education. They began realising that there was a future for them beyond mountains and bogs, so they left for Aberystwyth and beyond to find alternative work. So when good offers came from incomers, the crofters reluctantly surrendered their land. One by one they sold their heritage and retired down to Tregaron where the grass was greener, the earth softer and the slopes kinder to their arthritic joints.

Blaencaron, like dozens of similar Welsh rural valleys, began attracting incomers in the late sixties, when city dwellers and townies sought escape. Some longed to flee the smoke and the smell. Others yearned to escape the increasing city crime and overcrowding, or liberate themselves from the boredom of urban life. Some unashamedly blamed Asian immigrants for their need to escape. They accused immigrants of drowning their British culture, not realising that they themselves were responsible for overwhelming the indigenous culture of the Welsh heartlands.

The incomers could be placed into three categories. Firstly there were those who sought the 'good life'. These were followers of dreams, who left the cities seeking a small cottage by a stream with a few acres of land where they could be self-sufficient. They had idyllic visions of keeping horses, goats and poultry, living on their home-grown vegetables and, perhaps, practising a craft such as pottery, candle-making or wood-turning.

In a second category were the yuppies. These, unlike the good lifers, were fairly well-off professionals. They were early-retired business people: bankers, teachers, business executives and doctors. Like the good lifers they sought solitude and, in both cases, having placed their suburban homes on the market, they could easily afford to buy small cottages – or indeed substantial houses – tied to small parcels of land in the rural areas. The difference in house prices between the English cities and villages like Tregaron was immense. City sellers could, therefore, not only afford their dream cottage in the country, but also spend thousands on its renovation and still have a tidy sum left over in the bank for a rainy day. Little did they realise that there would be many such days in rural mid Wales.

Making up the third category were the hippies. These again were mainly urban folk or townies, mostly young people who had decided to spurn materialism and any form of ordered and outwardly respectable living. They were the spiritual adherents of the Haight-Ashbury flower people – the sons and daughters Bob Dylan had referred to who were beyond the command of their fathers and mothers. Many were transients, followers of pop festivals who, for short periods, would settle in tepees, benders or tents in obscure valleys. They dreamed of changing the world. But until the coming of the mind revolution, they were content to merely exchange their Giros for strong, cheap cider and cannabis joints.

Often there would not be a discernable distinguishing line separating the three categories. Some could be said to be a combination of two or even all three. Two of the main players in the LSD conspiracy, Richard Kemp and Christine Bott, could be described as a combination of good lifers and yuppies. When he was younger, Kemp had tended to lean to the right politically, according to police forensic profiles. But college changed him. He became a left-wing zealot who wanted to change the world, and believed that LSD was the key.

It was as medical students in Liverpool University that he and Bott met in 1965. Bott, from Surrey, graduated and became a general practitioner. Kemp, originally from Bradford, was a brilliant scholar graduating in nuclear studies and then concentrating on biochemistry.

They found their dream cottage in the upper reaches of Blaencaron. Penlleinau, meaning Headlands, was a typical stone-built two-bedroom country cottage standing in two acres of land, consisting of a meadow and a large vegetable garden. It backed on to the narrow track leading to the mountains, the ideal place for Bott to breed her goats. She also found work in the accidents unit at Bronglais Hospital, Aberystwyth.

Kemp and Bott shared a love of gardening and goats. They contributed funds towards the Glastonbury Festival. He supported Release, a charity dedicated to reform the drugs law and aid addicts. She was a member of the Soil Association and the Goat Society. Often, Bott would be seen driving her partner in their old, dark red Land Rover to and from Carno, near Newtown, an hour and a half's drive away. But they seemed to be typical newcomers: quiet, friendly when addressed and keeping a low profile.

Kemp and Bott were given financial assistance towards the £9,000 purchase cost of Penlleinau by a fellow doctor, Mark Tcharney. Bott contributed £2,750. (It is listed on the market at around £285,000 and is now occupied by a couple who breed Irish wolfhounds and are well aware of the dwelling's notoriety.) Tcharney was from London, a graduate of Cambridge University. He found work as a locum in Lampeter and found his dream home, Esgairwen Uchaf (The Upper White Ridge) a few miles away at Cwmann, near Lampeter. He bought it for £21,000 and settled down with his partner, Hilary Rees, also a doctor, less than eight miles from Kemp.

Only six miles from Penlleinau, at Llanddewi Brefi, Frederick Alston Hughes arrived as if out of nowhere. He settled down in Y Glyn (The Hollow), a terraced cottage in the centre of the village. A sociable, confident and outgoing character, he easily made friends. He was known as 'Smiles' on account of his ever-friendly face and flashing white teeth. So pleased was he by his nickname that he had it tattooed on his wrist. Hughes, originally from

Birmingham, eventually married his partner, Mary. He became a legend in the area.

Another hippy-type who moved to the village was Paul Healey, known as 'Buzz'. A very likeable man who still lives in the area, he married a local girl. They had two daughters and were a Welsh-speaking family. Indeed, Healey insisted that his children should receive a Welsh medium education.

Yet another hippy, Russell Spenceley, moved from Chatham to the hamlet of Maesycrugiau near Pencader. At the time there was nothing to connect him to Hughes, living half an hour away. Spenceley had lived at Reading and Woodstock. His wife, Janine worked as a nurse at Allt-y-Mynydd Hospital near Llanybydder and was well-liked. Spenceley loved good food and, unlike Hughes, lived the quiet life.

Richard Kemp's regular visits to Carno began to be noticed by the police, who were interested in an LSD production and distribution ring whose tentacles reached from London through the Thames Valley to somewhere in Wales. At the time they did not realise that the new owner of Plas Llysyn, Kemp's regular rendezvous, was a staunch disciple of the Brotherhood of Eternal Love. They were followers of Dr Timothy Leary, the new-age guru who promoted the use of LSD as a mind-expanding drug. Paul Joseph Arnaboldi had bought Plas Llysyn in 1974 for £25,000, with Kemp contributing towards the purchase. Arnaboldi had a persuasive cover, informing locals that he had bought the mansion for his mother, who lived in Florida. He was staying there temporarily, he said, writing a biography of John F Kennedy.

While working for an American construction company, Arnaboldi had been involved in a serious road accident. He received thousands of dollars in compensation which he used to buy a property in the remote village of Deia in the Tramuntana mountains on the south-western coast of Majorca. He had also enjoyed his fifteen minutes of fame appearing on television adverts as Captain Bounty, promoting the coconut chocolate bar of the same name. But there would be more fame – or rather more infamy – to come.

Hughes and Spenceley, together with Kemp, Bott, Tcharney and Arnaboldi, were to become prominent players in the coming police operation. Healey was merely a bit player in the game as Hughes' friend and occasional chauffer.

All these characters belonged to – or overlapped – all three categories of incomers. Such was the size of the influx, however, that normally they would have gone unnoticed. The numbers of incomers, transient and permanent, that came to the area can be gauged by the fact that during the early seventies a friendly soccer match was staged at Llanddewi Brefi. All twenty-two players who took part were hippies; and probably everyone who was watching. No-one remembers the score. To them, scoring had nothing to do with soccer.

2

GOD'S LITTLE ACRE

THE PARISH CHURCH OF Llanddewi Brefi is dedicated to Dewi Sant, or Saint David, Wales' patron saint. It used to be a place of pilgrimage, and some of the villagers still talk of the days when God was also an occasional visitor. He didn't wear long white robes or sport a flowing beard. But by Heaven, he could play guitar!

God visited Llanddewi Brefi after the arrival of a man who was both a hippy and a yuppie. For David Litvinoff, who heralded the hippy influx to the area, his rented riverside cottage known as 'Cefn-bedd' (Beyond the Grave) was a literal escape from London's most feared gangsters, Reggie and Ronnie Kray.

Crossing the Krays was not a wise move for anyone, as George Cornell and Jack 'The Hat' McVitie could confirm had they not been among the twins' fatal victims. There are various explanations offered for Litvinoff's spat with Ronnie Kray. Some believe it was to do with a rent boy. Others point to a drugs connection. It was, however, more likely to have been an unpaid gambling debt. There was mention of him owing the Krays £1,000. There were others who owed similar sums – and more – but had not been harmed physically. Why was Litvinoff singled out for punishment? We can only surmise.

Litvinoff's punishment was bizarre and yet typical of Ronnie Kray's methods of exacting revenge. Public humiliations were the preferred means. Litvinoff was, according to his own testimony, suspended by the ankles above the balcony of his flat. As he dangled there, tethered and helpless, Ronnie Kray flourished a sword and cut the hapless debtor from ear to ear. As it happened, an anti-nuclear protest was passing down the street right beneath him. And as the blood ran down his chin he could hear the protesters singing 'Corrina, Corrina', an old blues song revived in the sixties by folk singers including Bob Dylan.

It had been a close shave in more ways than one. He later left London and found refuge at the cottage on the south bank of the Teifi river, a mile and a half from Llanddewi Brefi. It was owned by a member of the Powell family, Brigadier General Percy Powell, Chelsea, once of Nanteos Mansion near Aberystwyth. Another member of the gentry who was friendly with him was Lord Bath, who ran a fashion business in London. He visited Cefn-bedd occasionally. Litvinoff was immediately accepted by locals as an eccentric but harmless hippy and bohemian. He was outgoing but had an obsessive aversion to having his photograph taken. He was also very wary of the police and the press.

His unconventional behaviour appealed to the locals. He always wore a rough collarless flannel shirt, much favoured by local farmers and shepherds. But rather than tuck the shirt into his trousers he would wear it outside, like a smock. On warm summer days he would sunbathe naked in the garden, music blaring from a speaker hanging from an apple tree connected to his record player. On one occasion he stripped off and performed a dance in a neighbouring farmer's slurry pit.

He would visit various farmers markets at Lampeter and Carmarthen, returning with gifts for his neighbours. He once bought a dozen frying pans and distributed them around the local households. On another occasion he encountered a charity walk aimed at raising money for Brondeifi Unitarian Chapel, Lampeter. Litvinoff joined them and their minister on their pilgrimage.

It soon became apparent to the locals that Litvinoff had some well-known friends when members of the Rolling Stones began to visit him. Mick Jagger's brother Chris also spent some time at Cefn-bedd. Litvinoff intimated that the younger Jagger had been sent to stay with him because he had encountered certain problems back home. One of the Stones, presumably Keith Richards, was interested in buying a mansion near Lampeter. A leak to the press put paid to this plan.

Richards in particular, who would arrive in a top of the range Porsche, would call in for a drink in the village pubs, the Foelallt and the New Inn. One day Litvinoff was collecting his mail from the village post office cum shop while a hired car waited for him on the village square. In the shop were a number of local women. Litvinoff told them to go outside and look into the car. He had with him, he said, none other than Cliff Richard. The women excitedly crowded around the car only to return quite disappointed. The passenger, they complained, was not Cliff Richard. They were right. He was the bemused Keith Richards.

Meanwhile, among callers at Cefn-bedd were John Lennon and Yoko Ono, who spent the night in a neighbouring village, Pontrhydfendigaid. Jimi Hendrix was also a visitor. Soon the news that pop stars were regularly visiting Litvinoff reached the local weekly paper, the *Cambrian News*, based at Aberystwyth. They sent down one of their reporters to make inquiries. Litvinoff teased him mercilessly telling him, 'Yes, the Stones have been calling. But you've missed the scoop of your life, man. I've had God staying here.' The reporter returned empty-handed and convinced that Litvinoff was a complete nutter. However, he was telling the truth. 'God' had been there: Eric Clapton would occasionally stay in a nearby cottage, Pentre Richard.

In his autobiography, Clapton omits any mention of Llanddewi Brefi, but he does refer more than once to Litvinoff. When Clapton was with Cream, Litvinoff was among the crew that frequented the Pheasantry in King's Road, Chelsea. Clapton once lived on the top floor there and the place attracted all kinds of celebrities. Litvinoff had told him that he had worked in Fleet Street ghosting the William Hickey column on the *Daily Express*. 'He had a vast knowledge of music,' says Clapton, 'which gave us a lot in common, and he was very funny, with his humour usually directed against himself.'

He remembers walking with Litvinoff down the King's Road and making a comment regarding a particular shirt he was wearing. Litvinoff's reaction was to rip it off from under his jacket.

'We would sit in the local café, the Picasso, and he would character-assassinate everybody who came in,' says Clapton. 'He'd go up to people he'd never met before and launch into a diatribe about them, pointing a finger in their face and telling them what they did, where they'd come from and what they were doing wrong. Then he'd turn the whole thing back on himself, as if to redeem the person he'd been attacking. He was absolutely extraordinary, and I loved him to bits.'

Some locals are convinced that Bob Dylan spent a few weeks with Litvinoff at Llanddewi Brefi. There was certainly a connection. Through a mutual friend and on the strength of my interest in music he invited me down to meet him. I had promised him that I would not publicise my visit. He had just returned from the 1969 Isle of Wight festival and had brought with him a tape recording of Dylan's complete set. He claimed that Dylan appeared on stage there wearing the suit that Hank Williams wore on the night he died, adding that the hypodermic needle last used by Hank still hung on one of the sleeves. With Litvinoff it was difficult to separate fact from fiction. Yet he seemed serious when he claimed that it was he, not McCartney, who had composed 'Yellow Submarine'.

He was the first person I ever met who would tape all his telephone calls. He replayed for me a conversation he had made with Dylan. He also played me a three-way conversation he and Dylan had made with an eccentric vagrant called John Ivor Golding, a London Welshman on whose character Harold Pinter reputedly based Davies, his eponymous 'Caretaker'. This is confirmed by Clapton in his autobiography, a revelation made to him by Litvinoff himself. Golding was another oddball who frequented the Pheasantry.

Local youths, who would congregate on Gogoyan Bridge near Cefn-bedd to chat on summer evenings, are still convinced that Dylan was the quiet young man who would join them there, leaning on his bicycle and listening with great interest to their Welsh language conversations. To them he was known as 'Jerry'. And when one of the youths, who worked as a farm-hand near Cefn-bedd saw the cover of *Nashville Skyline*, his reaction was to comment: 'Damn, I didn't know that Jerry had made a record.'

'Jerry' would often be seen walking Litvinoff's Labrador Jack to and from the village shop cum post office. (Jack was later wrongly reported for killing sheep and Litvinoff was ordered by Tregaron Magistrates Court to have him put down.) 'Jerry' would also be seen chatting with gypsies on the common. It is believed that he stayed in the area for around four weeks.

When I visited Litvinoff, I was amazed with his collection of half-inch tapes. There were hundreds on shelves lining the walls of his front room. Music was blaring and Jack would just lie there with one ear on a speaker enjoying the noise. Among his tapes was a recorded conversation he had made with Brian

Jones just a few hours before the former Stone died. Jones died in suspicious circumstances in his own swimming pool in July 1969. The conversation lasted up to an hour, and during it Jones revealed that a girl he was in love with had left him. He also revealed which drugs he was on at the time. The tape should have been central in the evidence presented at the dead Stone's inquest. But to my knowledge, the existence of the tape was never made known to the authorities.

Around a year later, on 18 September 1970, Litvinoff lost another close friend when Jimi Hendrix died. When I visited Dave a few days later he showed me an invitation card to Hendrix's funeral pinned to the mantelpiece. On the front of the card was stuck a boiled sweet which he intimated contained LSD. Those who could not attend were expected to take the acid at the exact time of the funeral.

During his period at Llanddewi Brefi, Dave was working on the film *Performance* (starring Mick Jagger) as a dialogue coach and technical director. The cult movie depicts the dark underbelly of the London gangster and drugs culture. The central character is a violent, psychotic East-end gangster who is hiding out following a hit. Dave was invited to work on it because of his intimate knowledge of the Krays' empire. Filmed in 1968, it was not released for another two years because Warners, the producers, were so worried about the morality of even screening it. Indeed, they considered destroying the negatives. It took many cuts and extensive dubbing of Cockney accents – work carried out by Dave – before they were

24

satisfied that it could be released. Much of the film's subsequent cult stature is attributed to Litvinoff's contribution.

One of the stars of the film, Anita Pallenberg, Brian Jones' and later Keith Richards' girlfriend, was interviewed by Chris Sullivan of the *Independent* on 16 March 2007. Asked to comment on the film, she specifically referred to Litvinoff saying that Marianne Faithfull regarded him as 'a genuine Mob boss'. She went on to describe him as a great friend of Ronnie Kray. 'But really he was Donald [Cammell, the author/ director] and director Nicolas Roeg's passport into the underworld. He knew them and took James Fox round London to meet the real guys.'

Litvinoff disappeared almost overnight. The mutual friend who had been responsible for our introduction had noticed a police car parked nightly near Cefn-bedd. He casually informed Dave that he was being watched, although he did not specify who the watchers were. The next morning Dave was gone, leaving his precious tapes and other effects behind. He later died in London. The Kray Twins were by now under lock and key, and he must have felt it was safe to return. Soon after returning he apparently shot himself. The response from one who knew him well was that had he not topped himself, then someone else would have done it for him. Indeed, some believe that his death was not as simple as it seemed. It is rumoured that he was involved in an expose of someone at the time of his death.

There is nothing to suggest that David Litvinoff was directly involved in the illegal drugs trade, but he was certainly a seasoned LSD user. Indeed, he is said to have secretly dosed some unsuspecting respectable people including a gentleman of the cloth, whose visit happened to coincide with that of a policeman from a neighbouring village who was answering a complaint regarding Jack. The coffee he made for them was suspected of being laced with an additional ingredient to milk and sugar.

Llanddewi Brefi, long before *Little Britain* discovered 'The Only Gay in the Village' and even before an LSD ring was operating locally, was well known to the London in-crowd and its beautiful people. The visits by Keith Richards, Hendrix and Clapton, all self-confessed users of narcotics, as well as Hendrix's psychedelic LSD-based music, all add up to more than coincidence. So, eight years before Operation Julie, the area was known as a secluded drugs paradise. David Litvinoff, like John the Baptist, may have been the man who led the way that others would follow.

3

HIGH HOPES

LYSERGIC ACID DIETHYLAMIDE COMES under many names and in many guises. Popularly known as LSD, it is also referred to as L, acid, blotter, cheer, dots, drop, flash, lightning flash, liquid acid, hawk, Lucy, microdot, paper mushrooms, rainbows, smilies, stars, sugar, tab, mellow yellow, trips and tripper, amongst many other nicknames.

It is a Class A drug, even though it is non-toxic and non-addictive. It is manufactured in tablet or capsule form, and in liquid form it can be dropped onto sugar cubes. Often it is dropped onto tiny paper squares, making up a sheet like postage stamps or transfers that have pictures or designs on them.

Nowadays the most common form is the blotter, with miniscule drops dotted on squares of absorbent paper. Unfortunately there is usually nothing on the square to indicate the strength of the dose. In order of popularity among recreational drugs, according to a 1998 survey, LSD came fourth after cannabis, ecstasy and amphetamines. Today it has also been overtaken by cocaine.

LSD is probably the most controversial of all recreational drugs. No wonder it is referred to as the 'heaven and hell drug'. To its adherents, it is experience enhancing and mind expanding. Its opponents maintain it can lead to serious mental problems and can cause flash-backs weeks and even months after it is taken. Usually, its effect kicks in within an hour and the ensuing experience, known as a 'trip', can last for between eight and twelve hours.

Survey groups have discovered that of all recreational drugs, LSD is credited with causing more of the best experiences as well as more of the worst. The best experiences, commonly reported after tripping in a good environment such as a pop festival, are said to include spiritual insights, self-awareness, out-of-world experiences, visual hallucinations, a good feeling, intensity of colours, bliss, a sense of well-being, increases in energy, hilarity and mirth.

The worst experiences include bad tripping in the wrong setting, panic and paranoia, nightmares, over-dosing, losing control and confusion. Bad trips were more common among those who felt they were too young to experiment or who were unprepared for the experience.

LSD is based on ergot, a rye fungus. The effects of contaminated ergot are known throughout many cultures. It is believed to have been used in ancient rites in Greece. In *The Brotherhood of Eternal Love*, Stewart Tendler and David May state: '... a more malevolent side has dominated its history in the West. If ergot-diseased rye was unwittingly milled into flour, the contaminated bread could produce mass mental and physical disorders. Medieval chronicles tell of villages where many went temporarily mad, men were stricken with gangrenous limbs and women aborted. St Anthony was designated patron saint of ergot sufferers and the poisoning dubbed "St Anthony's Fire", after the charred appearance of the gangrenous limbs. Even in modern times, ergotism, the medical term still appears and there were epidemics in Russia in the 1920s.'

Discovered by Albert Hoffman and Arthur Stoll in Switzerland in 1938, it was initially aimed at treating people with mental problems. The two chemists were searching for a cure for migraine when they accidentally discovered LSD at the Sandoz Clinic in Basel. Hoffman decided to experiment further. In 1943 he accidentally swallowed a drop and experienced an intense psychological and personality change. As this was the 25th version he had created, he named it LSD-25.

Intrigued, Hoffman took some more, deliberately this time. He discovered that as little as the 250th part of a gram was sufficient to change his state of mind for some hours. He found himself in a world of fantasy and magic. He saw incredibly bright colours and previously unseen images, and witnessed extreme emotions. Subsequent users have described a jumbling of the senses: seeing music and hearing colour.

Unfortunately, some witnessed a down side. Some users believed that they had superhuman powers such as the ability to fly. This trait is widely publicised by opponents to LSD use. Other users are said to have become aggressive. It is also extremely potent. Some tabloid commentators have maintained that two bagfuls introduced into the water supply could paralyze the United States for eight hours. Conveniently, the size of the bags is never specified.

But it is true that it is so potent that it can enter the body through the pores. Breathing in the vicinity of LSD can cause problems, as some police officers involved in Operation Julie discovered. After three officers entered the London laboratory where LSD was manufactured and pulled up the carpet where spillages had occurred, they witnessed differing experiences ranging from an extreme high to hallucinations. It should be noted, however, that they suffered no lasting effects.

Richard Kemp was involved in at least six reported road accidents. Some occurred during times when he was producing LSD; though not, it should be emphasised, the fatal accident in which he was involved. But were all his road accidents coincidental? Was he just a bad driver? Or did working so close to the drug cause some of them? It is also known that he sometimes deliberately took LSD in an attempt at making his mind and body immune to its effects. Then again, the accidents could well have been the result of tiredness, as he was a prolific worker when involved with production.

Acid was first brought to the UK at the end of 1952. Dr Ronnie Sandison, a consultant psychiatrist at Powick Hospital, Worcester, was invited to tour Swiss mental hospitals and also visited the Sandoz laboratories where he met Hoffman. Having discussed the effects of the drug, he returned two months later with a box of acid ampules. At Powick, he tested it on 36 patients.

During the Cold War period, intelligence agencies were awoken to the possibilities of using acid during interrogation, for mind control as well as for large-scale social engineering. The CIA ran a programme known as **MKULTRA**, involving mind control, from the 1950s till the late 1960s. Tests were also conducted by the US Army Biomedical Laboratory. The government would administer, without consent, LSD to subjects and then perform a whole range of tests to investigate the effects of the drug on soldiers. Based on available records, the projects seem to have concluded that LSD was of little practical use for mind control and scientists moved on to other drugs.

These experiments did not become public knowledge until the 1970s, as the test subjects were not normally informed of the nature of the experiments, or even that they had been experimented upon at all. There are rumours of a CIA agent introducing synthetic hallucinogen into Paul Robeson's drink in the singer's Moscow hotel room in 1961, leading to Robeson attempting suicide.

In August 1951 the villagers of Pont-Saint-Esprit in the Rhone Valley suffered what seemed to be collective madness. They saw visions, some ran around screaming, there were subject to numerous assaults. Even the animals went berserk. Five people died and virtually every family among the population of some 4,000 inhabitants was affected by what seemed to be lunacy.

The blame was attributed to a local baker. He was accused of using contaminated rye flour bought from a government-controlled mill. The same cause was attributed to the Salem hallucinations that led to the witch trials of 1692.

Recent research, however, has pointed the finger at a renegade CIA agent who decided to test the effects of LSD as part of a covert operation mounted by MKULTRA. The agent, Sidney Gottlieb died in 1999.

Most of the MKULTRA records were deliberately destroyed in 1973. As a result, President Gerald Ford created the Rockefeller Commission that introduced regulations on informed consent.

The British government is also said to have engaged in LSD experiments. During 1953 and 1954, scientists working for MI6 dosed servicemen in an effort to find a truth drug that could be used during interrogations. As in the case of the CIA, the test subjects were not informed that they were being given LSD, and had in fact been told that they were participating in a medical project to find a cure for the common cold. One subject, who was 19 at the time, reported seeing vivid images of melting walls, cracks appearing in people's faces, eyes melting and running down cheeks, Salvador Dalí-type faces and a flower turning into a slug. Like the CIA, MI6 decided that LSD was not a practical drug for mind control purposes.

After keeping details of the trials secret for many years, MI6 agreed in 2006 to pay the former test subjects financial compensation. Three UK ex-servicemen were paid compensation of under £10,000 each. Some were not informed of the nature of the tests for fifty years.

Whatever its dangers or merits, LSD was the 'in' drug during the 1960s. This was the drug of Flower Power, Haight-Ashbury, anti-Vietnam activists and civil rights protests. LSD was going to change the world. It was the drug of peace, of Love not War. Ironically, it was discovered the same year as the atom bomb, a fact emphasised by Hoffman. For the first time, mankind was capable of destroying itself completely. A new direction was needed, and many believed acid was the answer.

When America sneezes, Britain usually catches a cold. This time the opposite was the case. The psychedelic element of LSD was highlighted by a British medical expert, Dr Humphrey Osmond, a Harley Street psychologist. Indeed, it was he who coined the word 'psychedelic'. America soon caught on with the aid of Dr Timothy Leary, a lecturer in psychology at Harvard University. He had already experimented with mind-expanding substances, but as soon as he experienced LSD, he knew that this was the drug for him.

Leary gave up his academic post and moved to Millbrook, a huge mansion at Poughkeepsie near New York. It became the centre of Leary's cult, the Brotherhood of Eternal Love. His disciples took to the streets preaching the cult's message. It was Leary who coined the slogan: 'Turn on, tune in, drop out.' The Brotherhood became an umbrella movement for all sorts of cults and societies including, incredibly, groups that fostered violence such as the Hells Angels and the Weathermen.

It was discovered that one of Leary's closest

disciples was one David Solomon, an author who happened to have been a student at Cambridge and knew Richard Kemp. However, it should be pointed out that there was no direct link discovered between Leary and Kemp despite police attempts – sometimes desperate – to prove otherwise. The link is at best tenuous, at worst non-existent. But the media, especially the red top newspapers, have always dragged in the Leary connection whenever LSD is mentioned.

LSD was made illegal in the US in 1967, but Britain was open for LSD producers to legitimately manufacture the drug and then export it to the US. One company in Hampshire traded openly by mail. A similar company, Alban Feeds, was set up in Dunstable by the Brotherhood of Eternal Love to produce and market the drug for the US under the guise of developing livestock feed for the Third World. This was followed by another bogus company, Inland Alkaloids. The Brotherhood invested $100,000 in the venture. The two main figures behind it were Michael Druce and Ronald Craze, who went significantly further by illegally exporting the raw materials for producing LSD to the US.

The authorities on both sides of the Atlantic at last woke up to the fact that huge sums of money were being made from exporting and importing both LSD and the raw materials for its production. It seems that it was its money-making potential rather than its dangers that first prompted the authorities to act.

Operation BEL was set up in the US to counteract

the trade. Numerous LSD laboratories were discovered in California. Leary, described by President Richard Nixon as 'Public Enemy No 1', was arrested and jailed for ten years. He managed to escape, however, and the Brotherhood of Eternal Love paid $50,000 to a secret organisation to smuggle him to Algiers. He then went on to Switzerland, where he wasn't welcomed, so he moved on to Afghanistan. He was free for three years before he was re-arrested.

The international nature of the London and mid Wales LSD gangs' connections surprised the Operation Julie officers. One much-travelled operator was a mysterious character called Ronald Stark. He was imprisoned in an Italian jail having been found guilty in 1975 of being in possession of narcotics worth £45,000. He was sentenced to 14 years and was doing time at Bologna prison.

Documents placed by Stark in an Italian bank yielded some important information. Named in the documents were Kemp and Solomon, the former by now living in Tregaron, and Solomon, at the time, back in the United States. The documents also showed that Stark had been cooperating with the Sicilian Mafia in smuggling drugs into Italy hidden in stolen cars.

Stark's activities and motives, even today, are the subject of much speculation. During the early days of the Brotherhood of Eternal Love in 1969, he presented himself to them together with a whole kilo of acid. He was known to have flown to Britain to meet Kemp, providing him with an estimated 7.4 kilos of ergotamine tartrate, enough to produce 8.5 million doses of LSD. He is thought to have personally produced 20 kilos, enough for 50 million doses.

Stark went under different aliases – Khouri Ali and Terrence W Abbot being among them. He professed to have infiltrated the Palestinian Liberation Organisation and the Red Brigade and to have been a paid agent of the CIA. He may well have been a CIA agent, probably working on a freelance basis. When he was in jail he was regularly visited by a member of the American consulate. He spoke six languages and was known as an adventurer and an opportunist. The announcement of his death from a heart attack was greeted with scepticism. It was suspected that he had been given a new name and had disappeared. One thing is certain – if Stark was a CIA agent, it would not have been the first, and certainly not the last time the agency involved itself in illegal narcotics. Stark is regarded by many as having been an *agent provocateur*. Others believed him to have been a fantasist. He could have been both, but he was also undoubtedly a central figure in the global narcotics trade.

Then there came another international connection. A man known as Gerald Thomas was arrested at Montreal Airport by Canadian Mounties and was found to be in possession of 15 pounds of cannabis. Under Canadian law he received a life sentence. Rather than spend the rest of his life in jail, he offered information for a reduced prison term. His plea was accepted and his sentence was reduced to 15 months. After spending just seven months in jail he was extradited to the United States, where he was extensively grilled by narcotics police. He revealed that he had visited Britain in 1974 where he had worked closely in producing LSD with four others. He named them as Kemp, Bott, Solomon and a man known as Henry. He added that Kemp had been involved in the production of LSD as early as 1970.

There must have been some credibility in Thomas' confession. Following the arrest of the leading players in the conspiracy in 1977, some openly stated that they had been betrayed by Thomas and that they had put out a contract on his life. The police believed this was true. Kemp especially looked upon Thomas as a traitor.

Meanwhile, the information incriminating Kemp and Bott accumulated. Records were discovered mentioning the arrest of a carrier in Australia in 1974. The man, who wasn't named, had been apprehended carrying 1,500 LSD microdots. Like Thomas, he also managed to strike a bargain. As part of his confession he mentioned an LSD laboratory that existed somewhere in Wales. He also revealed he had obtained the acid from a London restaurant, the Last Resort, run by a man called Richard Burden.

The international nature of the operation was compounded during surveillance at Plas Llysyn in Carno, where Arnaboldi lived and where Kemp was a regular visitor. One day the watchers spotted an odd-looking stranger who called to see Arnaboldi. They recognised his accent as being American and he was later identified as Vladimir-Petroff Tshomakov, a fugitive from the Washington police. Having been accused of manufacturing LSD in the US, he was allowed bail at the sum of $50,000. But he had decided to skip bail and to flee to Wales.

Many of the suspects now under constant surveillance had international connections. Some were found to have safety deposit accounts in German and Swiss banks. Kemp and Bott travelled extensively throughout Europe. In 1972 they visited Norway. Arnaboldi regularly commuted between his home in Carno and the US and also had another home on Majorca. Alston Hughes visited Holland and India. Tcharney had visited Greece and North Africa. Spenceley had visited Europe, Scandinavia, USA and North Africa.

Then there were other operators whose names were yet to surface. Henry Barclay Todd, the chief London operator, had visited France, Denmark, Czechoslovakia, Malta, Berlin, New Delhi, Senegal, the US, Sierra Leone, Spain, Kathmandu, Canada, Greece and Barbados. Czechoslovakia was the main source for ergotamine tartrate, and Todd had lived there for six months during 1968 and '69. Between 1969 and '70 he is known to have spent £50,000 on travel.

Brian Cuthbertson, who became Todd's right-hand man, had a home in the Dordogne and had travelled throughout Europe, North America, North, West and Central Africa and the Caribbean. Andrew Munro, Todd's chemist, had visited Europe, North America, Mexico and the Canary Islands. Nigel Raymond Spencer Fielding, one of the main distributors, had been to North Africa, Europe, India and North and

South America. Distributor and money courier Martin William Annable had been to the Canary Islands and Portugal. The international connections seemed never-ending.

During the three years leading up to the creation of Operation Julie it is estimated that some one million tabs of acid were produced and distributed in Britain. The strongest and purest acid originated somewhere in mid Wales. Since 1972 it had been noticed that LSD was changing its form. Instead of acid-impregnated sugar cubes or blotter squares, buyers were being offered miniscule pills no bigger than a pinhead. Richard Kemp had perfected a way of crystallizing the chemicals and produced microdots in eight different colours. So minute were they that ten thousand of these domes, dots or volcanoes, as they were known, could fit into a matchbox. They were sold for as little as 50 pence and every microdot was 200 micrograms in strength, a microgram being one-millionth of a gram.

In 1976 and with Operation Julie in position, Dick Lee was aware of four important pieces of knowledge: there was a definite LSD connection between the UK and the US; the LSD market had tentacles stretching throughout the world; there seemed to be a connection between Richard Kemp, Roland Stark, Michael Druze, Ronald Craze and a man called David Solomon, who in turn was associated with Timothy Leary; and that someone in Wales was instrumental in the success of the illegal LSD trade.

It was obvious that Operation Julie involved two highly dedicated and intelligent factions. On the one side was the cream of the police forces. On the other side, some of the keenest of university brains, including old Cambridge colleagues Richard Kemp and David Solomon, were lined up against Lee and his squad.

As for Hoffmann, the man who started it all, acid did not seem to have had a detrimental effect on him. He died on 30 April 2008, aged 102.

4

CHASING SHADOWS

OPERATION JULIE WAS SET up only after a protracted and often bitter battle between the head of the Thames Valley Police Drugs Squad, Detective Inspector Richard (Dick) Lee and Scotland Yard's Central Drugs Intelligence Unit (CDIU). Lee had been puzzled by reports from the Windsor and Reading music festivals indicating a sharp rise in incidences involving the use of LSD. The average annual seizures of LSD usually totalled some 20,000 tabs. Yet reports indicated that the manufacture and use of this hallucinogenic substance was considerably higher.

Pop festivals were one of a number of bi-products spawned by the hippy culture of the sixties. They became a haven for drugs dealers and users. Organised affairs, such as the Reading Festival, were difficult enough to police. Free festivals, such as the one held in Windsor during the early seventies, were almost impossible to observe and police. Those attending these festivals would argue that no policing was needed, and that a police presence exasperated rather than calmed the behaviour of the devotees.

The 1974 Free People's Festival at Great Windsor Park, in particular, led to widespread rioting. There were over 500 arrests in four days and some 800 officers were deployed to bring the festival to a premature end. The violence wasn't all one-sided. There were 255 allegations made against the police, thirteen of which were substantiated. Questions were raised in parliament and an inquiry instigated. In order to combat such disorganized events, the local chief constable initiated the Stop the Unlawful Free Festivals (STUFF) campaign, consisting of six officers who would go underground, infiltrating those involved.

In his book *Busted*, Martyn Pritchard, who was recruited as a member of STUFF, pulled no punches in branding those responsible for these free festivals as 'deliberate criminals who were planning several ways to flout the law'. He went on, 'The people running the festivals believed they were untouchable, and by 1975 they weren't far wrong. So for my money, Operation STUFF was a success, not that year maybe, but subsequently when the background reports on this anarchy movement stuffed the free shows.'

The Watchfield Festival of 1975 held on an old airfield near Swindon saw more undercover officers operating than at any other free festival to date. It was meant to succeed the Windsor Festival and was held on 23-31 August 1975. Among the officers was Pritchard, who admitted to being frustrated at not being able to arrest any dealers.

In December 1974 Lee visited the CDIU and revealed his findings. The CDIU was housed in Scotland Yard's HQ and stored all information on drug dealing and drug abuse. It was also responsible for providing drugs intelligence to both the

Metropolitan Police (Met) and all provincial forces. It was, however, fiercely loyal to the Met.

The Met was well aware of the rise in the use of cannabis. But it seemed trivial compared to other social and political problems. There were a continuing and increasing number of IRA bombings in the capital and few resources for tackling the cannabis problem. With unemployment running at almost a million, cannabis use seemed a comparatively minor problem for the public in general. As far as the CDIU was concerned, LSD was also a minor problem. Lee, however, believed that the CDIU was well aware of the danger but chose to ignore it. His request for more manpower and funding towards forming a multi-force squad fell, therefore, on stony ground.

Later, Lee would discover that a director of the Home Office laboratory at Aldermaston had discovered through one of its scientists that there were similarities between microdots seized in the USA, Australia and South Africa, and doses made somewhere in Britain since 1971. Despite changes in shape, size, colour and ingredients there were definite common factors. Moreover, both CDIU and the Met knew of this evidence but, for reasons best known to themselves, had decided to keep quiet.

Was there a sinister motive behind CDIU and the Met's reluctance to act? In *Acid: The Secret History of LSD*, David Black concentrates on Ronald Stark's shadowy presence in America, the UK, on the continent, in the Middle East and Asia. To Black, Stark was central to the LSD story. Were Stark's connections with intelligence agencies on both sides of the Atlantic a factor in the CDIU and the Met's inaction? Was there an order from above to keep the lid shut tight on what was a veritable Pandora's Box?

Like the Met, British government officials had behaved as if either blissfully unaware of the extent of LSD production in the UK or chose to ignore it. Only three months before Operation Julie officers swooped, a World Health Organization conference was assured that no LSD was being manufactured in the UK.

Despite the Met's rebuttal, Lee refused to give up. He had already accumulated some useful evidence while investigating the cannabis trade. Two undercover officers, Martyn Pritchard and Andy Beaumont, had managed to infiltrate some of the gangs. In the spring of 1975 Pritchard had been offered a consignment of cannabis resin for £6,000 when the gang member casually asked him whether he was interested in buying acid. He was shocked when he was offered 1,000 tablets for £250.

Pritchard, a Welshman serving with the Thames Valley Police Drugs Squad, was well used to working undercover, infiltrating groups of dealers and users in pop festivals and college communities. During his investigations he came across a dealer called John Redfearn (Lee referred to him as Peter Harries) and set up a meeting with him and two others in a Reading car park. Police officers lay hidden nearby. As the deal was completed Pritchard was asked whether he wanted more. When asked how much he could supply, Redfearn's answer stunned him: 10,000 LSD tablets a week.

Pritchard arranged another meeting at the same spot and same time the following week. The gang arrived with £12,000 worth of cannabis and 1,008 LSD microdots. The hidden officers then pounced and arrested the pushers. They also made a show of arresting Pritchard. Redfearn was released on bail in the hope that he would lead them to the LSD source. However, he jumped bail, fled Reading and was next located at a hippy commune near Tregaron. This was the first intimation of a definite Welsh connection.

The suspicion that an LSD ring was operating in the UK was given further credence when Pritchard, having had his cover blown during the court case that followed the Reading success, went undercover in Chippenham. There, at the Bear Hotel, he befriended a man he referred to as Woodrow (Lee used the name David Smith, a pseudonym). Woodrow was a builder who seemed to be able to supply LSD in large amounts. Some of his customers belonged to the Let It Be hippy commune nearby.

Having gained Woodrow's confidence, Pritchard asked him of the possibility of obtaining LSD for some French hippies who had settled at the commune. He was surprised to learn that he could buy acid at £300 per thousand and that he could be supplied with anything up to 80,000 doses. These would sell for £1 each on the street. He knew that the largest seizure of LSD in the UK at the time was just over 32,000 tabs and that total seizures by customs and police around the world was 80,000. He was told by Woodrow that the deal could be ready within three weeks. Pritchard played for time, making the excuse that it would be difficult for him to finance such a deal at short notice.

Pritchard was intent on tracing the man behind the deal and following the chain. But Woodrow had no previous record, so he hit a dead end. Then Pritchard was told the deal was off because Woodrow's contact was no longer interested. Ultimately he got to meet up with this contact face to face in a flat in Frome, Somerset. He was known just as Alan (Lee uses the pseudonym John Lewis) and had Welsh connections. Unfortunately a visitor to Alan's flat seemed to recognize Pritchard so he was forced to pull out. Later, when Pritchard was working undercover in London, he was assigned a flat. Unbelievably, Alan stayed there and they renewed their contact.

Despite not being able to follow Woodward's chain of command further than Alan, Pritchard had gained some useful insight into the LSD situation. It confirmed reports from all over the world pointing to the existence of a big LSD production unit in the UK. This was confirmed by a London informer. Indeed, the informer had divulged useful information to the CDIU five years earlier. He had included names of some of those involved. But when Operation Julie officers asked for the files, there was nothing to see. The only remaining evidence was a file of transcripts between the informant and his interviewers, held by Thames Valley Police.

Eight of the Let It Be commune were later jailed for a total of 14 years for conspiring to sell Moroccan cannabis. John Redfearn, the dealer who had fled to Wales, stayed with some friends at a hippy commune in Ysbyty Ystwyth, ten miles from Llanddewi Brefi. He was arrested by officers of Dyfed Powys Police, including Richie Parry, following a car chase. He appeared at Aberystwyth Magistrates Court and was confronted by Martyn Pritchard, realising for the first time that Pritchard had been working undercover. Redfearn accepted the fact philosophically. In fact, on the way back to Reading, with Dick Lee's permission, Pritchard pulled up at a pub and shared a drink with his prisoner. The case was reported in the local weekly newspaper, the *Cambrian News*.

Following Redfearn's arrest, Lee immediately asked for officer Richie Parry's cooperation. Parry had knowledge of a Welsh LSD connection, telling Lee he had noted that the drug was cheaper to buy in Wales than England. The microdots in Wales were also larger, purer and stronger than normal. Following the Reading festival, convicted pushers confirmed that these particular microdots originated in Wales. In fact, their origin could be pinpointed to a village in west Wales. The stash of 1,008 microdots seized at Reading had been traced back to a house called Y Glyn in Llanddewi Brefi.

Indeed, LSD began to appear in the local area. At the University College of Wales' Welsh-language hall of residence, Neuadd Pantycelyn in Aberystwyth – where Prince Charles had spent a college semester six years previously – two students were arrested in May 1975 for possessing acid. The trail led to a dealer named as Frederick Alston Hughes. The nickname 'Smiles' also came up during interviews with John Redfearn. In fact, when Hughes had been interviewed by the local

Dyfed Powys Police he had been questioned about a man called Smiles but had denied knowing him. Little did the police realise at the time that they were talking to him. Hughes and Smiles were one and the same. This must have been hugely satisfying for Hughes and his bizarre sense of humour.

Hughes had a criminal record. Police files revealed that in the early '70s he had been involved in LSD dealing with Russell Spenceley. Hughes had convictions for theft and possession of cannabis. In 1973 he and his partner and her two children had moved to live at Y Glyn, Llanddewi Brefi. Then, in 1974, Spenceley had moved to live in Maesycrugiau, Carmarthenshire, a half-hour's drive from Hughes.

Parry then informed Lee that he had received information of renovations made by Hughes at his home. The work included fitting two hidden compartments in the walls that could be used for secreting drugs. Lee asked Parry to organise a raid on Y Glyn the following day. On Wednesday 16 April 1975 Parry, together with two of Lee's men, Martyn Pritchard and Bob Buckley, as well as members of the Dyfed Powys drugs squad left Aberystwyth for the half-hour drive to Llanddewi Brefi. With them, for his specialist local knowledge, was the village policeman Owen Lake.

They had only just left on their journey, according to Lee, when a colleague of PC Lake phoned the police station at Llanddewi Brefi. The constable's wife took the call and was asked to pass on a message to her husband. The colleague told her that her husband was on his way to Y Glyn. Believing that the matter was urgent she went over to Hughes' home, some 200 yards down the road, and asked him whether her husband had arrived. Learning that he had not, she asked a bemused Smiles to tell her husband to contact her when he did arrive. Hughes could not believe his luck. He cleared the house of any incriminating evidence and hid it in the quarry above the village. When he opened the door to the raiding party, his home was clean.

Now, it would be easy to mock the local police for what had happened. But this was the way things worked in quiet little villages like Llanddewi Brefi. Everyone knew each other, and the local policeman was an integral part of village life. But there is more to it than meets the eye. In an interview for a BBC Wales documentary televised on the 30th anniversary of the Operation Julie swoop in 2007, Richie Parry put a slightly different slant to the story. According to him it was Lee himself who 'foolishly' telephoned the village police station, leaving a message that he was going to be late. He added that the policeman's wife did only what any other village policeman's wife would have done. A rural policeman's wife, he said, was expected to act as her husband's unpaid secretary. Besides, PC Lake was not the sort of policeman to have been responsible for such an elementary mistake.

Whether the incident was concocted or at least much exaggerated, the supposedly botched raid was just the excuse the CDIU needed to go it alone. Some local cops felt that the incident was created by the CDIU as a means of keeping them and Lee's officers away. Whatever the truth, Lee was ordered to keep his nose out and to leave everything to Scotland Yard. Lee ignored the warning and was secretly pleased with the fact that the CDIU seemed, at last, to be taking the LSD threat seriously.

But Lee was amazed when the CDIU decided to ignore the possibility of a continuing connection between Hughes and Spenceley. Here were two men who had been involved in dealing in LSD together in London and Birmingham and who were now living within fifteen miles of each other. Yet the CDIU did not consider the possibility of a current link existing between them.

However, the CDIU came up with one important lead. The names of Richard Kemp and his partner Christine Bott had been known to them for at least a year, thanks to information from both Stark and Thomas, but they had not previously mentioned them. When they did, a bell rang loud and clear in Richie Parry's memory. He remembered that a man called Richard Kemp had been involved in a fatal accident some weeks previously. He had been driving his dark red Land Rover between Tregaron and Carno when, near Derwenlas, he collided with a car driven by the Revd Eurwyn Hughes who lived at Talysarn near Caernarfon. The collision resulted in the death of Revd Hughes' pregnant wife, Sheila. Hughes himself was seriously injured.

The accident had happened on Monday 14 April, just two days before the supposedly botched raid. Kemp appeared at Machynlleth Magistrates Court two months later and was committed for trial at Welshpool Magistrates Court, charged with causing death by dangerous driving. At the ensuing court case, Kemp was fined and had to forfeit his license for twelve months. Coincidentally, I was covering the inquest for the *Western Mail*, not realising that it would directly lead to cracking the LSD conspiracy.

Kemp's Land Rover, with a load of slates in the back, had already been searched as a matter of course. It was still impounded at the police compound at Aberystwyth, but Kemp had been allowed to remove all his personal documents from inside the vehicle. Now, a minute search of the vehicle's contents was made by Richie Parry, Noir Bowen and Trevor House. They removed the slates one by one. There, beneath all the pieces of slate and debris, was a rough map noting various locations and, more significantly, a torn piece of paper. When the pieces were joined, the handwritten words 'hydrazine hydrate' were deciphered. Hydrazine hydrate is an integral component of LSD.

It was now realised that Kemp's name had cropped up at various times previously. And in September 1974, following an earlier accident, he had made what proved to be a basic error. He gave police his defunct London address but handed in his driving documents at Welshpool police station, not far from Carno. Now the pieces and the names were falling into place: Kemp and Bott, Hughes and Spenceley were all living within a few miles of each other. They had discovered the Welsh acid ring. Or so they thought.

Now that Kemp had been located, a meeting involving officers of Dyfed Powys and Thames Valley Drugs Squad was held at Carmarthen to discuss a surveillance operation on both Kemp and Bott.

This was now a priority, as a well-known dealer from South Wales had been seen in Tregaron. But internal politics soon put paid to any concerted effort to observe and follow them. Any form of unilateral action was opposed by the CDIU, who jealously guarded their independence. Their refusal was admitted in a report included in a Home Office post-trial file. A request for permission to mount a surveillance operation was also refused by the Home Office. Although permission was later granted, little was done.

As for Lee, it had been a protracted and frustrating fight. At a conference at Swindon in February 1976 involving five provincial forces as well as Scotland Yard, the CDIU and a Home Office drugs inspector, his plans hit a brick wall. Scotland Yard refused to be part of any concerted operation against the growing problem of LSD.

But at a subsequent secret meeting five days later in Brecon, the chief constables of Dyfed Powys and North Wales Police, Richard Thomas and Philip Myers, refused to lie down. Both held other important posts and carried considerable clout. The former was chairman of the Association of Chief Police Officers while the latter was secretary of the association's CID committee. Having listened to Dick Lee's evidence it took them just fifteen minutes to put in motion the formation of a multi-force operation.

It was launched on 23 February 1976. Dick Lee was appointed commander of the operation and it was based in an old police driving school in Devizes, Wiltshire. Officers regarded as the cream of eleven forces were gathered together and a £2 million fund was allocated for the work. The task force's brief was to locate the illicit LSD laboratory, to identify and prosecute the persons running it and to identify and prosecute the major distributors. This would be the first time ever that an operation outside the control of any one force had been authorized.

Then there came another failure by the CDIU to cooperate. They refused to transfer their file of evidence on the use and production of LSD in the UK. When they were later forced to do so, Lee was shocked to discover that the CDIU had known for the past two years of the existence of an LSD manufacturing ring, referred to as the Microdot Gang in the UK.

Executive commander of the new squad was to be George Herbert of Avon and Somerset. He was highly critical of the inadequate vehicles to be assigned for the operation. He was also unhappy with the radio frequency allocated. The car-to-car frequency was right next to Capital Radio's and could easily be overheard. His complaints soon led to him being relieved of his duties. He was replaced by the deputy coordinator of the Bristol crime squad, Detective Superintendent Dennis Greenslade. However, in Lee's account, *Operation Julie*, the reader would be hard put to discover Greenslade's name at all. The book implies that Lee was running the whole show.

Meanwhile, the decision to form a specialist squad was vindicated. Home Office research into the proliferation of LSD showed that the ratio of microdots as a percentage of all acid seizures jumped from five per cent in 1971 to 80 per cent in 1975.

The next step was to choose the squad, all handpicked from the eleven forces involved. Eventually they would number 25 men and three women. At the initial meeting, chief officers were discussing possible code names when in walked Sergeant Julie Taylor from the Wiltshire force offering them all a cup of tea. Sergeant Taylor, a strikingly attractive girl, immediately turned every head. And thus Operation Julie was named.

5

THE STREETS OF LONDON

NOT FAR FROM THE square at Llanddewi Brefi, an old black and yellow enamel AA road sign notes the distance to London. It is securely bolted to a wall lest it should suffer the fate of other village signs stolen as souvenirs by fans of *Little Britain*'s Dafydd, supposedly the 'Only Gay in the Village'.

The distance from there to London is noted as being exactly 211¼ miles. From Llanddewi Brefi, as well as from surrounding villages just over a century ago, drovers walked their cattle to far-away markets such as London's Barnet Fair. Later, during the 1920s, dozens of local farmers left for the English capital to work in the dairy industry. Practically every dairy in London was either owned or leased by someone from Cardiganshire. In the 1970s, trading between Cardiganshire and London still flourished. But rather than cattle or milk, the trade was now in LSD. Police were unaware that acid produced in London found its way to Maesycrugiau and then to Llanddewi Brefi before finding its way back to London again having, during its circuitous journey, doubled or trebled in price.

The two production centres, however, had a common denominator: Richard Kemp. He had originally been responsible for the London production. But for some reason not known at the time he had decided to up sticks and to set up his own enterprise in Wales. He and his partner toured in a caravan before finding a temporary base in Carno, then a permanent home near Tregaron.

But who – and where – was the London connection? It was now obvious that Kemp had been the manufacturer. His connections went all the way back to David Solomon and Cambridge University. Time and again Kemp's name, together with that of his partner Christine Bott, emerged during enquiries.

Solomon was known to have been friendly with people known as just Henry and George when he was at Cambridge. The police suspected that Henry and George were one and the same person, and that he had a police record. Gerald Thomas had revealed such a detail. Records of all fourteen courts in the Cambridge area were examined to no avail. No appropriate surname could be added to either Henry or George.

At last a driving license provided the answer. Not only did it provide a name but also an address: Henry Barclay Todd, 148 Cannon Street, East London. Unfortunately, it was just a mailing address. Where, then, did this elusive man live? If he had a criminal record, he must have an appropriate address. Yet every document traced in his name mentioned Cannon Street. But then, secretive as he was, his impatience betrayed him. By chance, one of the officers happened to notice a passport application for Todd's daughter. He had left the application until almost too late. Therefore, so as not to lose valuable time, he entered his proper address. It was 29 Fitzgrove Avenue, at the back of Olympia. As a bonus he had also included his telephone number.

A surveillance team was set up immediately and soon the elusive Todd was spotted driving up to the flat in a Volvo Estate. But the watchers were at a distinct disadvantage. Not only did they have to drive up from Devizes every morning in their inadequate green van, they also lost valuable time finding a parking space nearby.

Todd seemed to have few visitors, but one day a tall stranger turned up. From the welcome he received it was obvious that Todd and his family knew him well. He was identified as a member of the Baader-Meinhof gang. He had been caught smuggling drugs through Heathrow and subsequently released on bail.

The Baader-Meinhof gang, at its most active during the 1970s, was a product of the West German student protest movement. It was a militant left-wing urban guerrilla group that became known as the Red Army Faction. During its 30-year existence it was responsible for 37 deaths, many of them being secondary targets.

It seemed that Todd had other German connections. He had an account with the Berliner Bank and one of his agents lived in West Germany where he was a distributor. But despite Todd's apparent opulence, he was living on state benefits.

During surveillance, Todd was heard talking on the phone to someone in the Dordogne. It was also discovered that he had applied for a Green Card, enabling him to drive in France. He needed insurance for a second Volvo car which, amazingly, was registered to Donald Sutherland, the well-known Hollywood actor. At the time he was in Rome filming *Casanova* but was found not to have any connection with drugs. Todd had merely used his name.

September 1976 was unseasonably warm and the watchers in the green van were made to sweat. Life for Todd seemed to be a routine. He dined out in expensive restaurants, often with a friend, David John Heasman, who himself became a suspect; he visited West End shows and took a holiday in the Dordogne. Then Todd began phoning various police stations in London. Had the watchers been spotted? No, but a friend had tipped him off that the police seemed interested in him. The friend, however, assured him that the police interest was no more than routine traffic inquiries.

Following this narrow escape the watching police were thankfully supplied with rooms in a building near Olympia. They were also supplied with brand new radios operating on a special channel that facilitated listening in to Todd's telephone conversations. This soon brought dividends when officers discovered that a London policeman was being paid by Todd for information.

Then there was a sudden burst of activity suggesting the completion of a new batch of LSD. Todd was overheard ordering radio equipment from a specialist firm and mentioned an address: 23 Seymour Road, Hampton Wick. The house was registered to J J Ross and had been bought for £33,500. Ross was yet another of Todd's assumed names. The house was watched.

With the team being stretched, four extra officers were recruited to keep watch, two at a time. Among the four watchers for six weeks, sometimes working a 24-hour shift, was Noir Bowen from Dyfed Powys Police. He was one of fourteen officers billeted at RAF Hendon. During surveillance duty, he and another officer had to share a nondescript van with blackened windows that included the luxury of a porta-potty behind a curtain. Later they moved into a box room in a house overlooking Todd's house. Bowen recalls that his daily subsistence allowance was £3.75. Officers would pool their money into a kitty to buy food that they themselves cooked.

Despite the 24-hour watch, there was still no sign of a Welsh connection. Then the name 'Phil' cropped up and the information that he owned a 60-foot mast boat. Every boatyard in Wales was searched but no connection was made.

The existence of the Carno laboratory was now known but where the raw materials came from remained a mystery. Companies producing chemical apparatus were consulted. A buyer named Blunt was mentioned. It was yet another of Todd's assumed names. In fact he was found to have 21 different aliases. 'Blunt' was known to have bought colouring ingredients and glass apparatus suitable for producing LSD. The goods were being collected personally by Todd from Kings Cross station.

Then another stranger was spotted visiting the

Seymour Road premises. He invariably travelled on foot and by tube, buying tickets to Clapham Common and walking to Chessington Court at Forest Green. A policeman was assigned to track his moves. He was identified as Brian Cuthbertson, a known LSD contact.

Connecting Todd in London and Kemp and Bott in Wales became a priority. But all surveillance in both London and Wales was futile. There were leads but they led to dead ends, like the time when Todd was overheard referring to a Swiss company producing ergotamine sulphate, a basic chemical for the production of LSD. During this conversation he mentioned a visit to Bordeaux where he would pick up his new Volvo. Frustratingly for the police, he did no more than that. There seemed to be no links between London and Tregaron.

Officers began wondering how the business was run. Were production, tableting and distribution organised separately? Was it run on a cell system? Perfected by the IRA, the cell system was based on small groups – or even individuals – working separately towards the same end but with one cell not being aware of the identity of the next.

Then, officers in both London and Tregaron detected growing activity. Would there be a meeting at long last? And if so, where was the venue to be? Todd was buying more and more equipment. This time the equipment was secretly marked before leaving the company for later identification.

Despite not identifying the London-Wales link, more and more evidence was collected, so much so that officers felt that they could move very soon. Three teams were drawn up in advance of a simultaneous swoop on London, Carno and Tregaron.

In early March 1977 another name appeared. Todd was heard talking to someone in Edinburgh. Addressed as David, he was ordered to 'buy the CL' and bring it down to London. CL was calcium lactate, used in acid tableting. A check with the Post Office revealed the telephone subscriber as David Brown Todd, Henry's brother. He was subsequently spotted in London and followed to Seymour Road. The watchers had seen him three months previously but had failed to make the connection.

At Seymour Road, activities grew apace. Todd and Cuthbertson were seen loading plastic bags into various cars. They drove them to a dumping site near Reading. They then set the bags alight before driving off, but police managed to salvage some of them. They contained LSD microdots, traces of CL as well as tablet moulds. But there was nothing to connect the evidence to a tableting centre. On another nearby dump, LSD-making equipment was discovered. The equipment suggested a direct route to the manufacturing of LSD.

The time to swoop was nearing and the chiefs were getting impatient. Meanwhile, Todd was heard cancelling the daily milk delivery. He was also known to have booked flight tickets to the Bahamas. Would Lee's men have to arrest Todd and his cohorts before swooping in Wales? That was the last thing Lee wanted to do, since it would alert the others.

The file on Henry Todd was now practically

complete. Born in Dundee on 3 March 1945, he was the son of a high-ranking RAF officer. He attended school in Dundee, Singapore and Malaya, passing six O Levels and two A Levels. He left school to work as a porter before moving to Paris to work as a photographer. Then, back in Cambridge, he had been found guilty of theft and fraud. He was jailed for two years. He then worked as an accountant before moving to the Czech Republic. He returned after six months to his accounting, moonlighting as a nude model.

Police created a forensic portrait of Todd. A large man, he was portrayed as energetic, secretive, a fast driver, intelligent, a good organizer but with a suspected violent temper. He was a good rugby player who turned out for London Scottish. He was outgoing, interested in mountaineering and travelling, loved good food and attractive women. His politics were unknown. He was known to have safety deposit boxes in the Berliner Bank, Berlin. He was the common law husband of Maureen Ruddy and they had one child, a three-year-old girl. His motive was solely money. There was nothing in his file to indicate that he would soon be sentenced to 13 years in prison.

Todd and Kemp were two completely different animals. While Kemp lived frugally in his country cottage, Todd would enjoy dining at the Savoy Grill and Wheeler's and holidaying in the Bahamas. He invested in rare stamps, drove a top of the range Volvo and bought a similar model for his wife.

Police suspected that Todd and Kemp had

previously worked together, but they did not know to what extent they had been colleagues and collaborators. They seemed to have parted but this could well have been deliberate as part of the cell system that might be involved.

Gradually police began filling in the gaps. Kemp's role as Todd's London chemist seemed to have been filled by Andrew Munro, another ex-Cambridge graduate who had a Master's degree in chemistry and a home somewhere in Ireland. Munro had known Todd and Kemp from their Cambridge days. He had also been used by Solomon and Thomas in their attempt to synthesise cocaine.

In charge of tableting and distribution was Brian George Cuthbertson, the adopted son of a Birmingham magistrate and a Reading University drop-out who had failed his mathematics course. He officially lived in Grand Gouyas in the Dordogne, France. Despite being unemployed he was known to travel extensively and, like Todd, loved the high life.

A mysterious member of the conspiracy, known only as Leif, was pinpointed as an important dealer who was supplying a source in Wales. He was identified as Nigel Raymond Spencer Fielding – 'Leif' being the first part of his surname reversed. Fielding, born in Hanover where his father was an army officer, was an economics graduate from Reading University. He owned a health shop in the town where he had once studied.

Still perplexing, though, was the London-Wales manufacturing connection between Todd and Kemp. Lee's officers, time and time again, had followed trails that had come to nothing. What – or who – was the connection? The answer, when it was revealed, would shock even the most cynical officer. Indeed, it would shock some of the conspirators.

6

THE WATCHERS

TREGARON IS EITHER A small town or a large village. No-one is quite sure which. It depends on whether it is market day or not. One thing, though, is certain: its inhabitants do not suffer fools gladly. It is a no-nonsense frontier settlement, the last stop before crossing the Cambrian Mountains, once known as the 'Green Desert of Wales'. Hundreds of acres of sheep pasture have been covered with Forestry Commission evergreens and abandoned to soaring red kites and bare-legged, masochistic hill walkers and ramblers.

Lord Beeching closed the railway that used to connect the area to Carmarthen to the south and Aberystwyth to the north in the early 1960s. The station is now the local bowling club. The heart of the town is the Talbot Hotel on the square, standing behind a statue of Henry Richard, Apostle of Peace (1812-1888). As a Unitarian minister it is appropriate that he turns his back on the inn. A Tregaron man visiting North Wales was once asked by some locals where Tregaron actually stood. His answer was: 'Just outside the Talbot.'

When traveller and writer George Borrow was on his way to Tregaron in 1854, he enquired to a passing local of the nature of the place. His reply was: 'Oh, very good place; not quite so big as London, but very good place.' As he reached Tregaron, one of the inhabitants advised him to visit the Talbot, ' ... where they are always glad to see English gentlemen.'

Today at the Talbot, one of only two inns left in the village, you can learn anything from the price of potatoes to the weather forecast for the next three days. But you should never push your luck there. It is far healthier for a stranger to listen rather than talk, and they should never offer advice unless asked. Some of those who have tried to take the initiative have done so to their cost. Tregaron people usually get their retaliation in first. It is, however, a warm-hearted, welcoming place once you get known.

In the mid 1970s strangers were easily spotted. Incomers tended to keep themselves to themselves. Newcomers, especially the convivial kind, would therefore be treated warily. A stranger eager to buy a local a pint would immediately be suspected of an ulterior motive. The pint would be accepted, but the buyer would get very little in return.

Dick Lee moved to Tregaron on 28 June 1976. He was known to his staff as 'Leapy', after the pop singer Leapy Lee who had a No 2 hit in 1968 with 'Little Arrows'. Lee, previously a uniformed Crown Court officer at Reading, was described by Martyn Pritchard as 'a good guy'. He was 'balding, wearing a waistcoat and puffing a pipe'. No amount of disguise, said Pritchard, would have covered him on a raid. His manufactured persona at Tregaron, however, was perfect.

Lee was billeted in a small cottage, Bronwydd,

a mile up the valley on the mountain road from Tregaron. Less than a mile away had once stood Fountain Gate, home of Thomas Jones, or Twm Shôn Cati, Wales' most famous outlaw. During the late sixteenth century this Welsh Robin Hood robbed from the rich and gave to the poor. How he would have relished the irony of a policeman living on his patch.

Lee's cover story was that he was Richard Calvert, a London businessman and ornithologist. His wife had just died and he needed peace and tranquillity to recover from his sad loss. He ran his own business and various strangers who visited him were passed off as members of his staff. This was the story he gave to the owner, Mrs Margaret Jones, who lived with her husband Ieuan and their children at Tyncoed and rented out the cottage for £10 per week. In fact, the Jones' lived near Penlleinau and would pass Kemp and Bott's cottage daily on their way to Tregaron. Little did they realise that Bronwydd's new tenant was there to keep watch on their own neighbours.

To avoid the inquisitive eyes and ears of the postman, a box was installed at the end of the lane leading to Bronwydd where the mail was deposited. And to further convince the postman that he was the man he professed to be, Lee would write letters addressed to his alter ego.

A man who moved in with 'Calvert' was described as his business partner. In fact he was Dave Redrup from the South Wales Police Force. In a place still 80 per cent Welsh speaking, Redrup's ability to speak the language was a distinct advantage. But he kept his bilingualism a secret. This would prove to be a wise move.

Both Lee and Redrup would visit the Talbot both lunchtime and nightly for a meal and a pint or two of the local brew. They were immediately accepted by bar manager Les Lewis. In fact, Les and Lee became good friends. 'He convinced me that he was an international businessman dealing world-wide in antique furniture,' said Les, who now lives in the Swansea area. 'I had no reason to disbelieve him.'

No-one was more surprised than Les nine months later when his mate Calvert was revealed to be an undercover police officer. 'I was working behind the bar when I saw, on the nine o'clock news, a familiar face. I called my wife over to have a look, and she was as surprised as I was. It was my old friend Calvert, now named as Dick Lee, talking about the raids. He was in Swindon at the time, but he later drove all the way to Tregaron to apologise to me for his lies. I liked him. He was good company.'

The Talbot was the perfect setting and the ideal cover for picking up any gossip. Customers discussing the two strangers would naturally do so in Welsh. On only their third night, Redrup overheard some of the locals discussing him and his 'boss', suspecting them of being homosexuals. The two had believed that they would soon become accepted. But gays were as welcome in Tregaron in those days as foot and mouth disease. So the following day a 'business secretary' arrived at Bronwydd. She was Glenice Garlick from the Thames Valley Police.

Lee's cover as an international businessman was

perfect as an explanation for his many absences. So, during the summer of 1976, when Lee's attention was diverted to Hankerton in Wiltshire, there were no questions asked. There, two dealers, John McDonnell and William Lochhead, had surfaced. They were believed to be responsible for supplying the cannabis, amphetamine and LSD sold in Glasgow and the Channel Islands. They often visited Malta and Amsterdam.

Across the road from where they lived was a row of diseased elms. Dick Lee came up with another good cover story for setting up a surveillance team in a nearby parked caravan He installed a team of 'students' from Bristol University who were studying Dutch elm disease. Among them were Dai Rees from the Dyfed Powys force and Glenice Garlick. Unfortunately the farmer who owned the land refused to cooperate. His reason? He disliked students.

So Martyn Pritchard was persuaded once more to go undercover as a pusher, using his assumed name Martin Poole. He happened to fancy McDonnell's sister which helped persuade the two dealers to accept him. Pritchard managed to buy 500 LSD tablets that had been produced by Kemp. By continuing to act as a dealer, Pritchard was taking a huge risk. Underworld intelligence revealed that a contract had been put on an officer by a wealthy industrialist from Stuttgart. The contract was worth £10,000 and the target was an undercover cop who had put paid to a cannabis ring operating between Mexico and Reading. The Mafia were said to be involved and an American had, apparently, accepted the contract. The target was Pritchard. Despite this he refused to withdraw.

McDonnell and Lochhead were known to be dealing in comparatively small amounts, around 1,000 microdots a time. But it was also discovered that they had contacts both in London and Wales.

A tap was placed on the two men's phone. During one conversation Lochhead was heard arguing over an order for 3,000 tablets. The supplier on the other end of the line was indignant. He would not concern himself with such a paltry amount. The reluctant seller was none other than our old friend Smiles from Llanddewi Brefi. He was obviously dealing in large amounts. A tap was immediately placed on his phone.

Meanwhile, Arnaboldi's house in Carno, Plas Llysyn, had been searched a month previously. Kemp was still a regular visitor and surveillance was operating from a caravan in full view of the house's occupants 24 hours a day. The caravan, a typical site office, was hired from a public works contractor. Five detectives took turns, passing themselves off as surveyors looking for coal seams in the area. Like Lee in Tregaron, they wrote letters to themselves so that when the postman called with mail, it reinforced their cover. Even a neighbouring farmer was convinced that the caravan was used by contractors. 'The yard where the caravan was parked was being used as a construction site,' said Huw Thomas in a television documentary. 'A nearby bridge was being rebuilt so I had no reason to suspect that anything out of the ordinary was going on.'

Arnaboldi would often be seen on the roof. By pretending he was replacing broken tiles he could view the area for miles around. A neighbour, the late Councillor Francis Thomas – Huw Thomas' father – told me that Arnaboldi's presence on the roof was a common sight. 'It was the perfect place for anyone wishing to observe anyone coming or going,' he said. 'He gave the impression that he was renovating the roof. I only realized after the arrests why he was spending so much time up there.'

If Tregaron could make an argument for town status, Carno was – and is – a village. Its main claim to fame is that of being the home of the Laura Ashley fashion empire that was, in 1976, preparing to move its headquarters from the social club to the old railway station. Laura Ashley, who died in 1998, is buried in the local church cemetery.

Plas Llysyn, a rambling mansion, is a prominent building on the edge of the village. Now and again the watchers would spot bail-jumper Vladimir Petroff-Tchomakov moving around. Although he was an American, his father was a Belgian diplomat. The fugitive spoke six languages and was considered by US authorities as a dangerous, armed man.

By May 1976 it seemed that the fugitive lodger had disappeared. He had probably been smuggled out. Lee was determined to organize a break-in to gather more direct evidence of where and how LSD was being manufactured. There was no time to lose. Kemp's behaviour indicated that another production run had been completed, while Arnaboldi was seen loading suitcases into his Mini Moke and leaving. He was on his way to his second home at Deia on Majorca. The mansion was empty. Indeed, the watching police were tipped off by a mystery woman who left a note in the caravan informing them that 'the American' was leaving for Spain.

Lee ordered Dai Rees and Terry Stokes to break in. They gained entry by forcing open a back window and by the light of a torch they searched the house's three dozen rooms. They were surprised to find that the interior was practically derelict. But they noticed that the door to the cellar was locked with a brand new padlock, which they unscrewed. Every room in the cellar, save two, was full of debris. The other two rooms, however, were spotlessly clean. Floors had been concreted over new-looking drains. An old chimney had been adapted for ventilation. A pile of dismantled wooden shelves were found that would later reveal important evidence. There were also two drums containing methanol residue, a chemical used in LSD production. The cellar, obviously, had been used as a laboratory.

The next step, after ensuring that no evidence of a break-in remained, was to obtain water and dust samples from the cellar. While examining an outside gully, a dead mole was discovered. Subsequent tests carried out on the rodent revealed evidence of LSD poisoning.

Meanwhile, Penlleinau was being watched from a holiday cottage some 200 yards away. There, at Tŷ Chwith, the watchers passed themselves off as fishermen. In order to be able to converse knowledgably with local and visiting fishermen they had taken lessons in the art of angling. Unfortunately there were no windows or door in the cottage's gable end facing Penlleinau so a hole was bored through the roof and a telescope installed.

Kemp and Bott's nearest permanent neighbours were Jack and Katie Davies, Penffordd. One of their daughters, Averinah, still lives there and well remembers the shock she and her family felt at the arrest of their neighbours.

'While the undercover police, unknown to us, were keeping watch on Penlleinau, my brother Glyn and myself would be out late at night hunting rabbits. We would be lamping – shining a powerful torch at the rabbits and catching them – while all the time the police must have been watching.

'As a family we were very friendly with Kemp and Bott, especially with Christine. She would often be walking past on her way to the mountain, sometimes walking the goats, and would always stop to chat to us. If she and Richard were away, I would look after the goats and would feed them. Richard was a little more reserved. He tended to stay in the background. When my mother died in 1993 I was both surprised and touched to receive a letter of sympathy from Christine. At the time she was living in the south of England.'

Another nearby cottage, Nantylles, was also used by undercover officers. It was owned by the same Jones family that owned Bronwydd, while the Davies family owned Tŷ Chwith as well as Isfryn, also used by undercover officers.

Previous to Arnaboldi's visit to Majorca, Kemp had

been driven regularly by Bott to Plas Llysyn where he would work for up to 48 hour periods at a time. He would then be driven back to Tregaron looking wan and tired. Then 24 hours later, he would be back in Carno.

It was obvious that production was in full swing at that time. Lee had been tempted to jump the gun and arrest Kemp, Bott and the two occupants. He knew that when current production ended, he would have to wait another year till the next production shift. Indeed, he was criticised in some quarters for not moving sooner. After all, if LSD was such a danger to its users, was it not a priority to remove this source as soon as possible? Lee, however, wanted to know more of the distribution chain.

At Tŷ Chwith, the holiday cottage near Penlleinau, the 'fishermen' left and another lot arrived, seemingly two young married couples. They, of course, were also undercover police. Luckily, among them was Noir Bowen, an experienced fisherman who was able to give the other three angling lessons and the use of his spare rods.

Attention now turned to Hughes. Llanddewi Brefi, like Carno, is a quiet village built around the parish church. The church stands on a small hill where, legend has it, St David once preached. A multitude of worshippers had gathered around, making it impossible for those on the fringes to see him. St David, it is said, caused the ground to rise beneath him and his church was later built there.

Hughes' house was a small terraced cottage opposite one of the village's two chapels. Rather than organise a surveillance team in one location, Lee opted for two officers to go undercover as visiting hippies. Such a ruse had already paid dividends when two of Lee's men, Martyn Pritchard and Andy Beaumont, had gone undercover as hippies – initially in London in April 1976 when they infiltrated student activities.

And so, Steve Bentley from the Hampshire police force and Eric Wright from Avon and Somerset arrived and concocted their own cover story. They posed as second-hand car dealers. They had come to Ceredigion to look for Wright's brother, who had joined a hippy commune. They had bought an old transit van which was also their home, sleeping in the back on two mattresses. They painted flower-power psychedelic images on the van. False driving licenses and criminal records had been prepared for them.

Although dressed as hippies, they fully expected to be suspected as undercover police. And they were. Gradually, however, they began to be accepted. Getting into a deliberate fracas with the village policeman helped their cause considerably. They befriended a hippy known as 'Blue', who was in turn friendly with Hughes. Producing a stash of cannabis worth £5,000 borrowed from the Bristol drugs squad clinched it for them.

In the meantime, Lee and Redrup, together with their company secretary, were ensconced at Bronwydd. Then came another development. Kemp and Bott were seen welcoming another couple as if they were old friends. They were Dr Mark Tcharney and his partner Hillary Rees. Tcharney had money invested in the purchase of Penlleinau.

Richie Parry discovered that the two visitors had bought a cottage just twenty minutes' drive from Penlleinau. It was an isolated dwelling called Esgairwen Uchaf at Cwmann. Dai Rees was sent to inspect the premises. It stood on an exposed hilltop but was hidden by trees, making it impossible to observe on a regular basis.

Tcharney, who had been at Cambridge University with Solomon and Todd, had paid £21,000 for the house. His previous accommodation was a London squat and his earnings would never meet the price of the house.

Then there came a blow: Plas Llysyn was put on the market. That meant the closure of the Welsh LSD laboratory. Was Esgairwen to become Kemp's next laboratory? Time would tell. But Lee had little time to waste.

7

BUGS AND TAPS

MERELY KEEPING TABS ON the targets through personal observation was not enough, since many of them were adept at spotting and losing suspected watchers. Kemp and Bott, in particular, were wary. Even before Operation Julie was instigated they had been rightly suspicious of local police interest. It was the opinion of Dick Lee that their fear of being arrested was behind their decision not to have children.

Christine Bott's interest in goats led her to entering two of them, Stella and Petra, in competitions at local agricultural shows. At Aberystwyth's Agricultural Show in July 1975, Petra was awarded first prize. Ray Daniel, a local freelance photographer attached to the *Cambrian News*, was present with his wife who helped him out occasionally. She took a photograph of Bott and Petra which the newspaper duly published. Later, it would be shown all over the world since it was the only current picture of Christine.

A member of the local drugs squad was alerted by the *Cambrian News* photograph. As members of the Dyfed Powys drugs squad did not possess a contemporary photograph of Bott, he approached the paper's editor and asked for a copy. The photographer was told of this request. But a friend of Kemp and

Bott who worked on the newspaper overheard the request and informed them of police interest. And so they were alerted.

In his account written by Colin Pratt, Lee got the following facts wrong. He names the newspaper as the *Western Mail* and also claims that Kemp and Bott were tipped off by the photographer. The same mistake is perpetuated in Tendler and May's *The Brotherhood of Eternal Love*. The photographer, in fact, could well have sued for libel. It should also be noted that the friend who tipped them off played no part at all in the illicit drugs scene. He merely shared Kemp and Bott's interest in goats.

Lee had realised from the very beginning that much more than merely observing and following suspects was needed. He needed bugging equipment as well as telephone taps. But this was a contentious issue even within the police themselves, who have invariably denied using such methods. Despite these denials, bugging and tapping have been common methods of collecting evidence since the late sixties onwards.

During 1979 and 1980 I was personally targeted. Arson attacks throughout Wales on English-owned second homes led to the formation of Operation Tân (Fire). Early on Easter Sunday 1980 there were widespread arrests. As a journalist working on a Welsh newspaper, I knew many of those arrested. On the day I was warned by a friendly officer to be very careful of what I uttered over my telephone. My phone was bugged. The police may have believed that relatives or friends of those arrested would have informed me and let slip the occasional clue.

Back in the 1970s an intercept necessitated a Home Office warrant, the permission of the local chief constable and a local magistrate's assent. All calls were then routed through Scotland Yard, meaning that the Met was the first recipient of any results.

Lee was criticized for revealing too much of police and Home Office bugging and tapping secrets in his account of Operation Julie. Lee and his co-writer Colin Pratt, however, refused to apologise. I feel that this was Lee's way of repaying the authorities for not perpetuating Operation Julie's activities. He felt betrayed, and it seems that he had good reason for feeling that way. The Home Office and the Met continually frustrated his requests for bugging and tapping devices.

They also considered the system to be both hypocritical and inefficient. They stated: 'The conversations overheard cannot be used in evidence. For example, a person may threaten to murder another on the telephone, and then commit the murder, but then the evidence overheard cannot be put before a jury. Conversely, when applying to the Home Office for an intercept, the police do not have to conform to any rules of evidence, but rather to satisfy the official that it is justified. In the USA, the enforcement agencies apply to a court for authorisation to tap by presenting evidence on oath as is necessary. Thereafter anything overheard is acceptable as evidence, both for and against the accused.'

As for meters, said Lee and Pratt, all British police had to do was satisfy a senior official in the Post Office Investigation Branch that the use of a meter was valid, but again, the records could not be used as evidence. In the USA, an application to the court enforced the telephone company to produce records of all calls made. These could also be used as evidence.

Lee and Pratt continued: 'The British Government does not officially admit that telephone taps exist, yet everyone knows they do. The police find them a tremendous help in combating crime and to dispense with this facility would seriously hamper them. Is it not time to put the situation on an open and sensible footing?'

When Dick Lee arrived in Tregaron in June 1976, his first task was to eavesdrop on Kemp and Bott. At the time, Lee believed that Kemp was just about to complete another production run of LSD. He knew that when this run ended, there would be a lull until the next batch was produced. So it became a game of cat and mouse.

Bronwydd, the cottage Lee was renting, is cradled by an elbow-shaped mountain. This blocked the view to Kemp and Bott's cottage in the next valley. Bugging Penlleinau would therefore involve sophisticated equipment. It would mean placing a transmitter on the mountain top and then running a light cable over a mile across open land down to the house. Radio transmitters were yet to be perfected. In case the officers were spotted, they had a ready explanation. As supposedly avid birdwatchers, they would explain to any curious passers-by they were recording birdsongs and sounds.

After an initial failure, the cable was laid. It proved impossible to bug Penlleinau itself because of the open ground in front of the cottage. However, as Kemp and Bott spent a lot of time in their garden, a microphone was hidden in the garden wall during the hours of darkness. As the device was placed the officers noticed that Kemp and Bott's bedroom window was wide open. They rode their luck and left unseen and unheard.

One day an officer listening in heard some strange sounds coming over the line. It was Welsh congregational hymn singing. Unfortunately, a passing sheep had taken a shine to the cable and had bitten through its insulation tape. This transformed the cable into an aerial that picked up Welsh-language programmes. The cable was soon mended and transmissions continued. Parts of the cable remain in place.

Lee's spats with the Home Office and the Met reached a head when the team heard of a tracking device costing £4,000 that could trace a suspect car without the pursuers having to keep the target within sight. This would make it far easier to follow Kemp and Bott's vehicle along narrow and winding country roads without being seen.

Lee felt that the device was a bargain and a necessity. He personally approached the Home Office with his request emphasising the Baader-Meinhof and Angry Brigade connections. He was given the go ahead. Dennis Greenslade secured the device and picked out a car that would be ideal as a tracking vehicle. He also examined a Renault 6 of the same model as Kemp's car and located a place where the transmitter could be fitted. But then came the bad news. The Permanent Under-Secretary at the Home Office personally blocked the move, as well as Lee's request for a sophisticated listening device to be placed within Penlleinau. The international connections that Lee had used in trying to persuade the Home Office to allow the device were turned against him. He was told that in no way was he to cause any possible international embarrassment to the government. Again, bureaucracy had raised its ugly head. If Operation Julie was to be successful, it would not be thanks to assistance from the Home Office.

Lee decided that he would not reveal the fact that he already possessed the sophisticated bugging equipment previously permitted and earmarked for Plas Llysyn. It had not been utilized because of the impracticability of installing it. The ground around the mansion was too hard to penetrate in order to hide the cables. So he decided to move the equipment and use it when and where he felt it was appropriate. For the time being, he would not approach the Home Office for permission.

Then, at last, fate was kind to Lee. Results of samples taken at Plas Llysyn proved that acid had been manufactured there. But he realized that to be successful, Operation Julie needed its own forensic expert. He was provided with the expertise of Neville Dunnett, a senior chemist at Aldermaston, where the tests were conducted. He wasted no time in getting into Plas Llysyn. Following cooperation from the estate agents he entered the building with Dai Rees and Terry Stokes. Dunnett noticed indentations in the walls indicating that shelves had been fixed there. The discarded laths found earlier were laser-tested for traces of LSD and proved positive.

There was an added bonus. Dai Rees discovered a water meter in an outbuilding. It was examined by the Severn Water Authority. Officers were astonished to discovered that over half a million gallons had been used during the previous 18 months. A normal family of four would have used around 45,000 gallons. They realised that the water had been used for distillation.

The action then switched to Penlleinau in Tregaron. Rees and three of his officers kept watch. Penlleinau had its back to the road and that rear wall had – and still has – only one small window. They considered inserting a bug in the window frame, but discovered that the cable would not fit beneath the guttering. However, a transmitter was modified and the problem seemed to have been overcome.

The plan was complicated. Kemp and Bott would have to leave the cottage long enough for the bug to be planted. Then officers on the hill above and others in cars would keep in radio contact in case they returned too soon. The two who were to place the bug would be given fifteen minutes to complete their work. A car would keep watch on the brow of the hill. Should anyone else approach, the two officers fitting the bug would pretend to be workers fixing the guttering. Should Kemp and Bott return too early, another car on the Tregaron side would stage an accident and block the road.

In essence, the plan meant fitting the miniature microphone into the window frame, its thin cable hidden in joints in the stonework. The transmitter and batteries, wrapped in a waterproof rubber tube, would be placed behind the guttering. It was a matter of watching and waiting.

Then, early one morning the long-awaited call came. Kemp and Bott were leaving. An unmarked police car in Tregaron watched the two leaving along the Aberystwyth road. A ladder was placed against Penlleinau's back wall. Then disaster struck. The cable could not be squeezed behind the guttering. Then they noticed that the bedroom window had been left open. This was an opportunity too good to miss. One officer climbed in and searched through cupboards and drawers. He copied various telephone numbers. Thirty minutes later, he was out.

They then decided to search an out-house. They could hardly believe their luck. There inside the door in a bucket were chemical dyes that could be used to tablet microdots. Samples were taken and the officers were ordered out.

Lee was in the United States searching through the files on mystery man Gerald Thomas. He just couldn't believe that such an intelligent man as Kemp would have left vital evidence in the open. It proved that Kemp had used his home as a tableting centre. Lee's luck seemed to be turning.

8

DOUBTING THOMAS

LEE FELT THAT GERALD Thomas could provide answers to many questions, so he flew to San Francisco armed with a copy of Thomas' file from the Royal Mounted Police. Thomas had apparently failed in an attempt to produce synthetic LSD and had therefore returned to what he did best – smuggling. He would discover that he was not very good at that either.

The information in the file detailed Thomas' arrival at Montreal on 3 June 1973 following a flight from London. He had secreted 15 pounds of cannabis in an airport locker before flying down to Boston in what was a dummy run. He was not stopped by customs. So he flew back to Montreal and picked up his stash and flew again to Boston, not expecting to be searched this time either. But this time he was stopped, his stash was discovered and he was allowed out on conditional bail, the condition being that he remained in Canada.

Six months passed and he then made a trade. For a nominal prison sentence – 15 months – he would pass on information on a British LSD ring. After only seven months he was released to the United States.

Lee's visit to the US was a historic event. It was the first time that the operational commander of what was, in effect, a British national drugs squad would work directly with a similar organization in the US. But he was not the first detective to fly out to interview Thomas. CDIU had previously sent out Detective Inspector Derek Godfrey together with Detective Inspector Charles O'Hanlon to meet him in Montreal in April 1974 – almost two years previously – and they had returned with some interesting knowledge contained in a comprehensive 15-page report.

This interview was the first clear evidence of Solomon, Kemp and Bott's involvement with LSD. Todd, back then, was only referred to as 'Henry'. Thomas referred to the fact that 'Henry' had a conviction, warned that he was keen to dilute and thus increase the number of dosages, and even provided an old address for him. Thomas identified the microdot gang's part in that first period of producing and distributing acid, their means of securing raw materials, Kemp's method of working, and the personal details and philosophies of Solomon and Kemp.

Godfrey returned with the information but by then Kemp, Bott and Solomon had gone to ground and 'Henry' was still unidentified. O'Hanlon was later jailed for eight years after being found guilty of taking bribes from pornographers while working with the Met's Obscene Publications Squad. Six Met officers had also been jailed for taking illegal payments from drugs dealers. This illustrates the chaotic state of the Met at the time. Even so, the CDIU saw fit not to release the gleaned information for two years.

The first stop on Lee's US trip was San Francisco,

where he aimed to discover a definite link between LSD operations in Britain and the Brotherhood of Eternal Love. Making that link had become his Holy Grail. At the time, the Drugs Enforcement Administration (DEA) was running a parallel campaign aimed at LSD production in the US, referred to as 'Centac X'. They made their files available to Lee.

The DEA has 227 offices throughout the US as well as 86 foreign offices in 62 countries. The most active office is in San Francisco, the city that is regarded historically as the LSD capital of the world. It had all begun there in the early 1960s, leading to 1967's famous Summer of Love. The city's Haight-Ashbury district became the centre of the hippy universe with its flower power and psychedelia. It still boasts its own Hippie Hill. From here it spread its vision of freedom, its fashion, music and drugs culture throughout the world. Ken Kesey and The Merry Pranksters, travelling cross-country in a school bus, organised concerts known as 'Acid Tests' where LSD was widely used both on stage and among the audience. (Kesey is best known as the author of *One Flew Over the Cuckoo's Nest*.) Despite the dissolution of the Brotherhood of Eternal Love in 1972, LSD still flourished in the States. Indeed, as recently as 2003 there were major prosecutions involving the production and marketing of acid.

Lee discovered that as soon as the Brotherhood had been dissolved, another organisation took over. Some of the personnel involved in the new venture had also been involved with the Brotherhood. Among them was the mysterious Ronald Stark. Most of those apprehended had been released on bail and many had decided to jump bail and disappear. But Centac X had already located two laboratories and had confiscated forty tons of chemicals and equipment. Here again, some of the people involved had been bailed and had fled. Among them was Petroff, the fugitive who was believed to have spent time at Plas Llysyn.

The DEA believed that LSD crystals were being smuggled in from Europe. Some were hidden in cases of wine sent from an area not far from Todd's chateau in the Dordogne. Worryingly, the DEA also discovered a link between the LSD venture and the illegal arms trade. And again the CIA seemed to have its grubby fingerprints all over the picture.

Lee decided to try and meet Gerald Thomas face to face. He left San Francisco for San Diego and then on to Houston, Texas. Thomas had covered his tracks well, but was eventually located. Lee arrived at his house unannounced. When he knocked and revealed his identity he heard the sound of running feet and a flushing toilet, before a very nervous-looking Thomas opened the door. No wonder he was nervous. He told Lee he had been a marked man for the past two years. His betrayal of his former colleagues for a reduced sentence had resulted in a contract on his life.

Thomas said that he was now free of the LSD scene and was legally employed as a chemical engineer. Over two days and a night he readily revealed his past involvement with Kemp, Arnaboldi and Solomon. He claimed that he and the two Americans had visited Millbrook, where the Brotherhood was based. Following Leary's flight from Millbrook in 1967, Solomon had left for England and Thomas for Baton Rouge. Until 1972 he had worked as a chemical engineer, initially for a legitimate company and then as a self-employed scientist, before leaving for England. There he chanced to meet up again with Solomon and decided that it would be cheaper to manufacture the chemical equipment there and export it to the US.

In Maida Vale he had met Kemp and Bott at Solomon's flat. Kemp was already manufacturing LSD and was interested in sharing some of Thomas' experience in large scale production. He had, in fact, shared a flat with Kemp for three months while Bott was away. There, Thomas had witnessed Kemp inhaling a dose of pure LSD as part of his research into the drug's effects.

He named others who were part of the scene including Arnaboldi and Todd. Solomon was the financier for the purchase of ergotamine tartrate, buying it under an assumed name in Laupheim in the German state of Baden-Württemberg and leaving it in a safety deposit box rented by Kemp in Geneva. He also mentioned Andy Munro, who tested the purity of LSD for Kemp at the University of East Anglia. This was to ensure that Todd was not diluting the acid for extra profit, suspicions that proved to be true.

Thomas believed that Solomon had shopped him to the Canadian authorities. In fact, Thomas had narrowly escaped arrest earlier when police had raided a flat he shared with Munro in London. Thomas happened to be away but suspected a tip-off, as the raiders had asked for him by name. There had been bad blood between the two of them because Thomas had tried to be over-friendly with Solomon's wife.

Before he left for Canada, Thomas had stored all his belongings, including notes on LSD production and equipment for converting cannabis resin into hash oil in a warehouse in London. Canadian police had discovered in his pocket a card bearing the warehouse's address. Fearing that they would pass it on to the Met, he asked Solomon to remove everything, as the evidence would have incriminated the whole ring. At first, he heard nothing. Then Solomon informed him that he had burnt everything. This meant a loss of several thousand pounds to Thomas. He was left with just the clothes he stood in. Upon asking Solomon for help he was told to 'get lost'. Enough was enough. Thomas threatened to expose the London connection and was then himself threatened by Solomon. Thomas ignored his threat, hence his decision to name him, Kemp, Bott and the man known as Henry.

To Lee, Thomas' confession was, like the proverbial curate's egg, only good in parts. He found it impossible to believe that Thomas, Arnaboldi and Solomon, having separated following the destruction of the Brotherhood, had just happened to meet again in London to form a new acid ring. Where did this leave Druce and Stark, who were believed to have been instrumental in setting up the London ring? But Thomas obviously did not want to make a connection between the Brotherhood and the London end.

Lee left with new insight but also many unanswered questions. How he must have cursed the

CDIU for not releasing its file earlier. This would have pinpointed the important names of those involved in the microdot gang from the outset. His predominant memory, however, would have been the experience of visiting the DEA's forensic laboratory in Washington. Among its collection of illegal drugs he was shown samples of LSD microdots produced by Kemp and Bott before 1972 in London, and later in Carno. He had much to ponder during his flight home.

9

A BAG OF BABY FOOD

IN OCTOBER 1976 LEE was back at his desk. New faces appeared in the Julie team. But it was two old faces that were involved in an bizarre unconnected incident. Eric Wright and Steve Bentley had completely gained the confidence of the man known as 'Blue'. So much so that he asked them to drive him to Speke Airport, Liverpool to pick up a friend, a Canadian boat dealer. According to Blue, he was coming over to buy a new boat.

The undercover men were given the green light by Lee. In Liverpool they met up with the Canadian, who was known as Bill Mandryk. Everything about him suggested opulence, from his expensive luggage to his drinking habits. During a long drinking session in a Liverpool bar, he revealed that his motive in buying a new boat was to adapt it for making drug runs in the Caribbean. He also revealed that he was interested in bringing cocaine into Britain.

That night, they continued drinking around Liverpool city centre, with Mandryk spending as if there was no tomorrow. The spree ended at 6 am. By early afternoon they were on the road back to Wales. Having already offered the two officers some valuable stolen jewellery to sell, Mandryk now revealed that he had come over to set up a cocaine distribution network in Britain. A partner in Bolivia was buying direct from source and they had recruited five beautiful girls, most of them ex-air hostesses, as couriers.

The officers were staggered when he offered them a stash of cocaine weighing 50 pounds for $23,000 per pound. This was by far the largest amount known outside South America and was worth $53,000 per pound on the street. By diluting it with milk, he revealed that he was raking in $64,000 a month, the money paid into a Cayman Island bank. The undercover pair showed interest.

Upon reaching Lampeter, the four men drove on to Bristol in a hired car. There Mandryk further revealed that he was involved in heroin dealing in North America. When they later revealed their experiences to Lee, they were told to stick with Mandryk and Blue. If Mandryk was truthful, and they had no reason to disbelieve him, this was big-time dealing. But as it was way outside the reference of Operation Julie, they passed the information on to other agencies. Blue and Mandryk then disappeared from Britain, but here was another international connection.

Back at Llanddewi Brefi, Wright and Bentley felt that they could not survive the coming winter in their battered old van. So, having been accepted as typical hippies they rented a house called Cartref not far from where Hughes lived.

Cartref means 'home', but Bronwydd, a few miles away at Tregaron, was anything but a home. There were only three beds to accommodate up to ten officers. At times, four officers shared a single bedroom and another four shared the dining room downstairs while Lee was allowed the only double bed in a separate bedroom. This was not because of his seniority. It was rather because of his snoring, which was legendary. The others used camp beds borrowed from the army. A single tap supplied water from an ice-cold spring above the house and washing meant utilising an enamel bowl. A three-ring gas stove provided the only cooking facility with the men taking turns to cook for the others. So bad was the cuisine that all the officers carried a stock of indigestion tablets.

Further stomach relief arrived in the person of Constable Alan Morgan from Avon and Somerset Police. He was appointed official chef following his very first offering of shepherd's pie made of corned beef, onions and potatoes, followed up by mincemeat flapjacks. His culinary skills excused him from observing Kemp's cottage from the top of the hill, a vigil that meant a two-hour shift for two officers.

Those vigils became almost unbearable with the arrival of arctic winds driving constant showers. The ground became so sodden that a spring appeared through Bronwydd's kitchen floor. Duck boards had to be placed on the floor as the water flowed out through the open door. Weatherproof army capes were obtained for the watchers on the hill above. There was a kitchen fire, but it was of little comfort as it continually choked on its own smoke and soot. Conditions got so bad that the two-hour shifts were halved. Ironically, Kemp was warmly ensconced in his cottage across the valley.

The situation must have rankled with Dick Lee. Here he was with his officers shivering less than a mile away and they were no closer to bugging Penlleinau. The break-in had proved to be fruitful but he needed more details regarding links in the chain. Two experts in Keith Campbell and Eddie McLean from the Devon and Cornwall force had been sent down to Bronwydd ahead of the new support team. As a rehearsal they decided, with Vince Castle, to pay a nocturnal visit to Esgairwen, believed to be Kemp's future laboratory.

The discovery of a black alkathene pipe running from the house to a stream seemed highly promising. Near one end of the pipe was an old water wheel, its channel choked with weeds. Dai Rees was then sent down to survey the site. He discovered the source of the water on the hill above. Esgairwen had formerly been a dairy farm, so a good supply of water was to be expected. It was also an all-important feature for LSD production.

Lee turned his attention back to Penlleinau. He had already decided that the bug would be placed in the ceiling of the first-floor landing. The transmitter would be powered with Kemp's own electricity. Alan Morgan would be taken off his cooking duties to place the device. Look-out and communication would be a repeat of the earlier successful break-in operation.

Lee was confident of success this time. Then calamity struck. Listening to the local gossip in the Talbot, members of the team overheard the rumour that Christine Bott had been temporarily employed to supply flu inoculations and would be away from the cottage for some time. This would mean that Kemp, his driving license having been confiscated, would be permanently at home. Bott had left in her Renault. Both her and her car had disappeared off the map.

The car was soon located by accident. While on another nocturnal visit to Esgairwen with the intention of mapping the house and surrounds, four officers were split into pairs. One pair inspected the outbuildings, in one of which they discovered Bott's green Renault. While inspecting the pipe discovered earlier they noticed that it was lying next to a brick-lined sump.

It seemed that things were moving at Esgairwen. But there was little the officers could do but wait and watch. Their vigils at the cottage were further complicated by Tcharney and Rees' acquisition of a pet dog that could alert the pair. Then came another blow. The surveillance team's customised Ford Cortina turned over on the way back from a visit to Carno. The electronic equipment in the boot was damaged and, even worse, the £6,000 aerial on the roof was broken into little pieces.

Despite all these setbacks, Lee decided that a permanent team in Wales was a necessity. They were, after all, tracking the movements of Kemp and Bott, Tcharney and Rees, as well as Hughes and Spenceley, within a ten-mile radius. Vince Castle, the experienced Gloucester detective, was joined by Pete Norton and Paul Purnell from Dorset and Bournemouth and Pauline Tilley from the Wiltshire Constabulary.

Meanwhile, Arnaboldi was back after spending

Christine Bott bred goats at her small-holding near Tregaron. Here she exhibits her goat
Stella at Aberystwyth agricultural show in 1975

© Raymond Daniel

Alston 'Smiles' Hughes, an LSD dealer who lived the 'hippy' lifestyle in Llanddewi Brefi.
© Raymond Daniel

David Litvinoff lived at Cefn-bedd, Llanddewi Brefi. An ugly spat between him and Ronnie Kray had forced him to uproot from London to Llanddewi Brefi.

© Raymond Daniel

Sergeant Julie Taylor from the Wiltshire Constabulary. Operation Julie was named after her.
© Raymond Daniel

Detective Superintendent Dennis Greenslade was executive commander of Scotland Yard's Central Drugs Intelligence Unit (CDIU), with Operation Julie officers searching Llanddewi Brefi quarry.

© Raymond Daniel

Detectives from the Dyfed Powys Police force who participated in Operation Julie, following the trial at Bristol Crown Court.

© Raymond Daniel

The morning of the swoop, and a mystery visitor is escorted from Y Glyn, Llanddewi Brefi by Detective Constable Gwyn Jones of the Dyfed Powys force.

© Raymond Daniel

Penlleinau was Richard Kemp and Christine Bott's home. Operation Julie police officers smashed open the sole entrance with a 14-pound sledge hammer before rummaging through the cottage in search of LSD. Police officers later even considered demolishing Penlleinau stone by stone.

© Raymond Daniel

Penlleinau, Blaencaron stood in two acres of land.
© Raymond Daniel

Penlleinau as it is today.

Reflecting the remoteness of this area of mid Wales, Penlleinau is situated just right of centre.
© Arvid Parry-Jones

Esgairwen Uchaf, Cwmann was the home of Dr Mark Tcharney, a London doctor and his partner Hillary Rees. Police officers believed that this was to become a laboratory for the production of LSD and would in time replace Plas Llysyn as a production centre. 50,000 LSD tablets were found hidden under a stone in one of the fields.
© Raymond Daniel

Plas Llysyn, Carno, the home of Paul Joseph Arnaboldi, which became a centre for the production of LSD tabs.

The cellars at Plas Llysyn. Most rooms in the cellar were full of debris, but two were spotlessly clean with concreted floors.

Bronwydd, a mile up the valley on the mountain road from Tregaron was the temporary home for police officers Dick Lee and Dave Redrup.

© Elizabeth Jones

At Bronwydd undercover police officers watched events at Penlleinau.
© Elizabeth Jones

Bronwydd as it is today.
© Arvid Parry-Jones

Nantylles, Tregaron was also used by undercover police officers.
© Arvid Parry-Jones

The Talbot Hotel, Tregaron: undercover police officers would regularly drop in for a pint in order to overhear local gossip.
© Arvid Parry-Jones

The Railway Hotel, Tregaron: a regular drinking haunt of a dealer called 'Doug'.
© Arvid Parry-Jones

Alston 'Smiles' Hughes and Russell Spenceley would set up meetings here in order to switch plastic bags full of LSD for money.
© Arvid Parry-Jones

The Ram Inn, Cwmann: the scene of other switches of LSD for cash.
© Arvid Parry-Jones

The Drovers' Arms, Ffarmers was another pub where 'Smiles' and Spenceley met up. On the 15th of December 1976, Spenceley entered the public house carrying a white plastic bag containing LSD worth £125,000
© Arvid Parry-Jones

four months at his Majorcan bolt-hole. He had been spotted at Heathrow and it seemed he was heading for Tregaron. He arrived there on 12 October and intelligence revealed that he was to visit an estate agency at Newtown the following day to discuss the sale of Plas Llysyn. He was followed by Dai Rees who managed to take his photograph. This was the first photographic evidence captured by the police of the elusive American.

Here, Lee admitted to a mistake. Rees was sent on his own to follow Arnaboldi. Unfortunately he lost him and the American made his way back to Majorca. A great opportunity was missed. Consequently, Arnaboldi was never arrested.

Then there came a much-needed breakthrough. The tap on Hughes' phone brought up the name of a John Preece from Birmingham. Officers would later discover that Preece had been married to Hughes' wife, Mary. Hughes spoke in code but he let slip that he would be posting something to a Birmingham address. The package was intercepted and was found to contain 500 LSD microdots. The package was then re-wrapped and sent on its way. This success was twofold: it proved conclusively that Hughes was dealing in LSD and it also broke the code he used.

This led to the interception of a second package sent to a London address which contained two quarter-pound packets of Typhoo Tea. They were delicately opened and revealed 1,008 microdots. The recipient was discovered to be an old friend of Preece and Hughes during their Birmingham days, a man called Tony Dalton.

The tap on Hughes' phone brought further success. Usually he only received calls, making it impossible for the listeners to locate the source. But he slipped up by phoning a man called Russ. Although they spoke in code, the man at the other end was discovered to be Russell Spenceley, the man Scotland Yard insisted had severed all contact with Hughes in 1972. It was now obvious that Spenceley was Hughes' supplier. Immediately, Dennis Greenslade applied successfully to the Home Office for permission to tap Spenceley's phone.

Meanwhile, pressure was being applied for an early conclusion to Operation Julie. A meeting of assistant chief constables in Devizes on 10 November 1976 gave them a mere three months' grace.

Hughes' phone was busy. Spenceley rang to inform him that he had '50' ready. This meant 50,000 tablets, valued at around £62,000, the largest stash of LSD ever recorded anywhere in the world. The highest seizure made at the time was 40,000 in Fenton, Missouri in 1973 from the Brotherhood of Eternal Love.

The two men discussed a location for a meet. It was decided that they should meet where Hughes and his partner had organized their wedding party. But where was this? Richie Parry at Carmarthen remembered that it had been held at the Ram Inn at Cwmann, Lampeter. Ironically, it was Mark Tcharney and Hilary Rees' local, being only a mile from Esgairwen.

Vince Castle was detailed to witness the transaction. With him he took Paul Purnell. He was warned not to make any move to arrest the dealer or buyer. The hand-over had been fixed for 6 pm. Hughes arrived five minutes early with his driver, Paul Healey. Fifteen minutes later, Spenceley walked in carrying a white plastic bag containing 50,000 tablets which was transferred to Hughes under the table. I later discovered from a source in Tregaron that the tablets were packed into re-sealed tins of Johnsons baby food.

Now Hughes' phone was red hot. Listeners heard another deal being organized involving Hughes, Preece in Birmingham and Tony Dalton. It seemed that LSD was to be exchanged for a stash of cocaine. Hughes, however, was unhappy with the arrangements and was driven to Birmingham by his friend Healey. He spent two days with Preece. The deal fell through, but another one materialised involving 20,000 tablets in Southampton.

The picture was still incomplete. The search was on for a man referred to by Hughes as 'Doug'. It became obvious that Hughes was keen to sell his stash as soon as possible so as to be able to pay Spenceley, and Doug was one of those buying from him. Lee's luck held once more. Bentley and Wright in Llanddewi Brefi heard of a man called Doug who was friendly with Elizabeth Taylor's son, Michael Wilding Jr, who lived on a farm at Ystumtuen to the north-east of Aberystwyth. (Wilding made headlines when his mother called to see him and took him out to dinner at Aberystwyth. He also appeared at Aberystwyth Magistrates Court accused of possessing cannabis.) Doug was thought to be in London at the time. But while drinking at the Railway

Hotel in Tregaron, Bentley and Wright started talking to a tall stranger. When Hughes and Healey later arrived they obviously knew the stranger and, to the undercover men's surprise, referred to him as Doug.

It was a Tuesday, market day when the pubs remained open (officially) all day. As the afternoon grew more boisterous and Doug got more and more intoxicated, he left the Railway Hotel and conveniently broke a shop window. He was arrested and had to reveal his name and address. His name was Douglas John Flanagan and he lived at 20 New King's Road, Fulham.

With Spenceley now a key figure, his home at Glynrichet Fach, Maesycrugiau became a focus of attention. But it was even worse than Esgairwen, with virtually no cover for observation. The Home Office's permission to tap Spenceley's telephone, however, compensated for that.

Meanwhile, things seemed to be moving at Esgairwen. Vince Castle had discovered that a filter had been placed on the end of the black alkathene pipe, the sump cleared and another pipe pressurised. And significantly, some of the outhouses were being renovated.

The tap on Hughes' telephone continued to pay dividends. On 15 December officers were alerted to another meet between Hughes and Spenceley, this time at the Drovers' Arms at Farmers, six miles from Llanddewi Brefi. This time the amount of LSD involved would be double what had been exchanged at the Ram Inn.

Farmers is a small village with only one pub

and can be reached along the mountain road from Llanddewi Brefi. Two sets of strangers appearing in the quiet bar simultaneously would draw too much attention, so the four watchers were told to conceal themselves within sight of the pub. One loitered in a nearby telephone kiosk.

The meeting was scheduled for 7 pm and Hughes, together with Healey, arrived just three minutes late. Eight minutes later Spenceley arrived in his Range Rover. He entered the Drovers' Arms carrying a white plastic carrier bag. In it was LSD worth £125,000. The officers then saw Hughes coming out of the pub and nonchalantly tossing the bundle in the back of Healey's Vauxhall.

Hughes' phone tap then revealed plans for the arrival of 100,000 tablets from Fielding. Hughes and Spenceley arranged another meet, this time at the Black Lion Hotel at Lampeter where another exchange was witnessed. Hughes had been joined in Llanddewi Brefi by Preece. Then Dalton arrived to spend Christmas with Hughes. It was obvious that the network was taking time off over the festivities. This allowed the Welsh police team a much needed break and the opportunity to spend Christmas with their families. On 23 December a party was organized in Devizes for the officers and their wives, girlfriends and boyfriends.

10

DOTS AND DOMES

LEE WENT BACK TO work on 3 January 1977 not realising that in three months' time it would be all over. Although the Welsh end of the operation seemed to be resolved, there was still no current connection between Richard Kemp and Henry Todd. Lee had exactly one month before the next chiefs' meeting, for which he needed to provide a completion date. He was confident that the new laboratory at Esgairwen would be in production by then. Already there were grumblings regarding excess overtime pay so it was imperative that he should have something concrete to tell the chiefs.

Lee felt elated when Vince Castle reported that a dam in the stream at Esgairwen, spotted before Christmas, had been built higher and the water course and the pond had been cleared. Also, the drain outlet for the sump had been discovered. It was obvious that work had been carried out over the Christmas period despite snowstorms and freezing conditions. His hunch that this would be the next lab seemed to be correct.

At Llanddewi Brefi, Wright and Bentley were thankful for the roof above their heads at Cartref. Although they had long been accepted by members of the hippy community, Hughes would still try to goad them occasionally by accusing them of being undercover cops. He did this again at the end of a long drinking session, but Wright had had enough. He pushed Smiles up against the wall and threatened to smash his teeth. Hughes apologised and never goaded him again. But true to his humour, he dubbed the two officers Reagan and Carter, the two main police characters in the TV series *The Sweeney*.

Then it was Bentley's turn to prove himself. When a local policeman ordered him one night to drink up after stop tap, he turned on the constable, much to the delight of Hughes.

Soon there came another example of the guile of the conspirators. Spenceley was heard, during a phone call to Hughes, referring to 'domes' being available rather than the usual microdots. This had happened as a result of the 'other man' picking up the wrong package. Domes, also known as pyramids, are rounded on one end, unlike microdots. They had been discovered before, but Operation Julie was concentrating on microdots, believing that this was the only form being produced in Carno and London.

Domes were largely meant for export. Microdots and domes were therefore believed to be produced by separate rings. But now it was obvious that both forms were being produced simultaneously. This, thought Lee, was down to Todd's intention of confusing the police.

But who was the 'other man'? He was, obviously, as high as Spenceley on the chain of command. Finding him could take time, of which Lee had little. The chiefs were calling for a completion date. When Lee presented his report on 2 February 1977, he stressed that almost the whole distribution network had been identified. Those involved in the production were under surveillance and the one laboratory (at Carno) and the potential lab (at Esgairwen) were being watched. Lee argued against moving until the new lab was operating. This would strengthen the case against the manufacturers, where the evidence was weaker than in the case of the distributors. He asked for 30 days' grace.

Meanwhile the logistics of the raid were revealed: over 800 officers using 350 vehicles would be involved in an area between Glasgow and Southampton. Seventy warrants would be executed and 120 people arrested.

The extent of such an operation would be a severe test of security and secrecy. Premises to be raided were located in several different police areas, so warrants would have to be obtained by several different magistrates. The danger of leaks was high. Additionally, the warrants would remain active for only 28 days. Any raids not executed at the time could involve warrants having to be re-sworn.

Lee left the meeting with the chiefs a very relieved man. His plea for an extension of 30 days had been reluctantly granted. But there was still much to be done and he knew that it was unlikely that the deadline would be extended any further.

Officers listening in to calls to and from Penlleinau were alerted by an enquiry by Christine Bott to British Rail. She enquired of the train times from Neath to

London on 7 February. On the very same day, Todd had ordered laboratory equipment. Where was Lee to concentrate his officers? He chose to watch Todd, and briefed Richie Parry from Dyfed Powys Police to keep an eye on Bott. He also briefed Special Branch.

Bott boarded the 12.14 London-bound train while Todd collected his lab equipment. Were the two scheduled to meet in London? No such luck. The following day, Todd collected some chemicals in metal drums. The drums were marked by watching officers.

Bott, on the other hand, had bought a British Airways ticket to Zurich. She had not pre-booked and she paid in cash. Lee immediately asked Swiss police for surveillance support. The Swiss detective in charge sent some of his men, in the guise of currency officers, to search her luggage. They discovered £16,000 in sterling and Dutch guilders. Her explanation was that the money was her and her sister's savings.

Following her to the Kantonal Bank the next day, the Swiss detective discovered that Bott and Kemp owned a joint account. Bott returned to Wales by ferry and train.

There was also a further development at Esgairwen. Work on clearing the water course and around the pond and the sump had been completed. Tcharney had been heard telling Kemp cryptically over the phone: 'The river runs slowly.' Interior work was another matter. Tcharney was also sighted making many car trips to an unknown destination across the English border. Later he was tracked to a cottage in the village of Calmsden near Gloucester.

Meanwhile, having gathered sufficient evidence against Hughes (who was still throwing his money around like confetti), the tap on his phone was removed and replaced on Fielding's line in Reading. Lee then decided to pull Wright and Bentley from Llanddewi Brefi. Their work was done. They had wormed their way into Hughes' friendship and even baby-sat for him and Mary, thus being provided with total access to the house. Their cover story was that they had been offered work on the south coast, but they kept up their pretence with the occasional return visit to the village.

By now there was a tap installed on Cuthbertson's phone in the Dordogne. But bureaucratic delays by the French police rendered the operation worthless. It was decided, therefore, to send a member of the Julie team over to listen permanently to the taps. The officer chosen was Dai Rees from Dyfed Powys Police.

Meanwhile, Todd was busy buying lab equipment and various chemicals, shopping around and travelling hundreds of miles so as not to alert the authorities.

But the ends were being tied up. The tap on Fielding's phone brought up the name of Martin William Annable, formerly of Reading University, a teacher at a girls' school and the courier between London and the distributors. And a name from the past surfaced, that of Richard Burden, an acid dealer who ran the Last Resort restaurant in London. Indeed, there was a reason to believe that Burden had international connections. He was a known acquaintance of Izchak Sheni, who had bases in London and Amsterdam and was suspected of smuggling LSD and other drugs to the continent and Israel.

The raids were now pending. Briefing centres were organised for Aberystwyth, Carmarthen, London, Reading and Birmingham. A file was prepared on each of the premises to be raided, including photographs of the targets and the interior of their locations. Equipment such as hammers, forks, spades, protective clothing and vehicles was provided for every raid.

As HQ, Swindon was given preference over Devizes simply because it offered more cells – enough to house the 50 or 60 prisoners that needed to be handled simultaneously.

Timing was to be of the utmost importance. Once the raids began, news would quickly spread enabling some of the conspirators to escape. So meticulous was the planning that all those to be arrested were allocated their interrogators in advance. The most intelligent of the conspirators, Richard Kemp, would be questioned by Graham Barnard of the Thames Valley, aided by Peter Spencer from Hampshire. Barnard was himself regarded as being both highly intelligent and patient. Christine Bott would be paired with Eddie McLean, chosen for his friendly, sympathetic manner. His back-up would be Devina Blackstaff of the Gloucester Constabulary. And so the matching went on. Interestingly, Wright and Bentley were spared the task of interrogating Hughes because they had become so close. Lee didn't want them compromised. The task was given to one from outside the operation, Richie Parry of Dyfed Powys who had crossed swords with the enigmatic Hughes before the advent of Operation Julie. Interestingly, Lee himself decided to tackle Todd, the man expected to be the hardest nut to crack.

Then, with everything poised to go, HM Customs threw a spanner in the works. They had been shadowing a man called Frank John Manocheo. Living in Maida Vale, Manocheo was an American fugitive from justice in connection with a huge cocaine shipment. The cocaine had been sized by the DEA and Manocheo had fled.

Lee was reminded of the proposed deal of LSD for cocaine attempted by Hughes and Dalton two months previously. Customs officers had spotted both men visiting Manocheo in London. As a result, they had made plans to raid Hughes' home. They were about to do so when a colleague of Lee arrived in the nick of time. Lee wanted to have Manocheo arrested and interrogated as he suspected him of being involved in smuggling LSD into the United States. Customs, however, demanded priority and Lee had to stand by. However, it could have turned out much worse had they raided Y Glyn before Operation Julie swooped.

Then there came another blow, something that Dick Lee had long dreaded. The planned operation was leaked to a national newspaper. A senior reporter on the newspaper contacted a customs official and revealed to him that he knew of a hunt for an LSD laboratory and that Dick Lee was in charge. He had received his tip-off from someone at the Watchfield pop festival.

Dennis Greenslade, armed with a hidden recorder, met the reporter at the customs official's office. He needed to know the source of the leak. Unfortunately he was not given the chance to properly switch on his recorder. The meeting, however, continued with the reporter correctly detailing his knowledge of a police team operating in Wales out of Devizes. Greenslade managed to persuade him to agree to postpone publication.

Lee subsequently listened to the recording, which was of poor quality, and came to the conclusion that the leak had come from the London end rather than from one of his own officers. The reporter proved to be true to his word and nothing was published until after the arrests.

No sooner was one security leak plugged than another possible leak threatened the operation. Just nine days before the scheduled raids, the sale of Plas Llysyn, to the background of a falling-out between Kemp and Arnaboldi, was in the balance. The buyer somehow heard of police interest in the sale, and although work had started on renovating the building, he threatened to pull out. This angered Kemp. He blamed Arnaboldi for the delay and the fact that no money had been paid up front as a deposit. But there seemed more to the quarrel than the sale of Plas Llysyn, and to the listeners it seemed that this would mark the end of their association.

Phone taps had indicated that the potential buyer was to meet with the two men to discuss the sale further at the Newtown estate agent's office. The last thing that Lee wanted was for Kemp to make a public scene of dissent, thus drawing unnecessary attention to himself.

Lee decided to contact the buyer and to lay his cards on the table. They arranged to meet at the mansion where, realising the importance of secrecy, the buyer decided to cooperate, promising that he would sign the deal for the £18,000 sale within the next few days. Lee took the opportunity to look over the cellars. Parts of the house were already being gutted and he was told that the cellars were to be turned into flats. The prospective owner, however, promised to delay the work for a few weeks. The methanol drums, spotted earlier by Rees and Stokes, remained and Lee knew that some wooden staging had been removed by Kemp and taken to Penlleinau. When Lee left, he took the drums with him.

But with Todd still buying equipment and chemicals, Lee was caught between the devil and the deep blue sea. What did Todd have in mind? Was he stockpiling with a view to moving to a new production centre at Esgairwen, while Munro and Cuthbertson were still tableting the products of the previous run? Or could it be that there was no connection between Kemp and the London team?

If tableting was still ongoing, Lee knew that it would take some six weeks to make 20,000,000 doses of acid. Then there came another quandary. The microdots and domes seized during recent raids, believed to emanate from the same source, were now suspected of being produced by two different laboratories. They varied in quality. While the dots were practically pure, the domes contained an impurity known as iso-LSD. This was the first intimation that Kemp and Todd were running two different LSD rings.

Lee came to the conclusion that there was – or had been – a lab at Seymour Road after all and that Esgairwen was, as he had suspected, being prepared to replace Plas Llysyn as a production centre. Lee needed even more time. And he got it – seven extra days.

11

ASSISTING WITH ENQUIRIES

AT PRECISELY 5 AM on the morning of Friday 26 March, Lee's officers were to swoop on 87 different premises. At Seymour Road, however, it was decided to strike ten hours earlier. Three of the conspirators were known to be there, as well as Maureen Ruddy, Henry Todd's common law wife. But as Todd had cancelled the milk and made plans to leave for the Bahamas, Lee was afraid to risk waiting till the scheduled time in case the birds had flown.

So, at 7 pm on Thursday 25th the house was stormed by 14 officers and secured. Officers gained entrance by smashing through the French windows at the back while another group burst in through a side door. The telephone was ripped off the wall to avoid any warning calls – in or out.

Lee greeted the handcuffed Henry Todd who was totally unfazed. His opening words were: 'I suppose you've come about the television license.' He then asked whether the police had come to present him with the Queen's Award for Industry. As his pockets were turned inside out, a cigarette lighter was found. It was a gift from Dolder Ag, the Swiss company that had been supplying Todd with ergotamine tartrate.

Todd accepted the situation stoically, as did Munro

and Cuthbertson. Meanwhile, officers were searching the premises. Lee was inspecting some plastic bags in the hallway when he was called upstairs. He climbed to the second floor and saw the elusive acid laboratory set up in two bedrooms. Observers had dismissed any thoughts that it was located there, overlooking the street with the curtains rarely drawn. In a bedroom on the floor below evidence of tableting was found.

According to Martyn Pritchard, the camp had been split over the question of a laboratory at Seymour Road. The basement had been cased from the outside and Lee had stated categorically: 'No way is there a lab at Seymour Road!' At the farewell party following the end of the trial, he was presented with a plaque which read:

NO WAY

ITALASR

There were more interesting discoveries. Various cereal cartons contained cash totalling £20,000 and 250 milligrams of LSD, enough to produce 2,500,000 microdots. The trio of Todd, Munro and Cuthbertson were thought to have used 15 kilos of ergotamine tartrate to produce an estimated 30 million microdots.

Not all the busts were as dramatic. Pritchard, in charge of entering Fielding's home at Reading, knew that the place was empty. Both Fielding and his wife, Caroline were visiting the Spenceleys in Wales.

At Penlleinau, Barnard led his crew into Kemp and Bott's well-tended garden before smashing in the door, the house's sole entrance, using a 14-pound sledge hammer. Bott's sad comment was: 'I don't suppose that I'll be digging my garden for a few years now.' It seems that Kemp was not taken unawares. He later told the police: 'When we were busted, frankly I was not surprised. We had had many warnings in the previous couple of years but I had rationalised them all away.'

At Esgairwen, Vince Castle and his team were in place early on Friday morning about a mile from the house. They slipped quietly along the lane to the cottage. At Llanddewi Brefi, Richie Parry and his team were to enter Y Glyn, the home of his old adversary, Alston Hughes. Other teams were standing by in Birmingham and various addresses in London while Dai Rees was in charge of entering Cuthbertson's chateau in the Dordogne.

Various premises yielded their secrets. At Dalton's flat in London, 50,000 microdots were discovered in a packet of Scott's Porage Oats. Annable's flat yielded 26,000 Dutch guilders. At Penlleinau, Kemp's safety deposit box key was discovered. At Cuthbertson's chateau there was only one occupant, a Welshman. He was reluctant to talk. Rees, on an impulse, addressed him in Welsh telling him that he had better come clean. It worked. The man became most cooperative. But it was soon obvious that he was not connected to the LSD conspiracy. Rees, however, discovered Cuthbertson's French bank account and evidence of a safety deposit box.

Esgairwen yielded something quite unexpected. No trace of a potential laboratory was discovered. But a call had been made from there informing someone in

London, who had an American accent, that Tcharney had been arrested. The call was found to have been made to none other than Timothy Leary's dedicated disciple, David Solomon. Within a few hours he was arrested and taken to Swindon.

The interview process was long and involved with Todd refusing to admit to anything. Others, however, yielded information in dribs and drabs. Spenceley admitted being involved for the past six years. Hughes admitted having been dealing in LSD for the past three years. Kemp admitted manufacturing LSD and of having a safety deposit box in Zurich. Fielding admitted his part as a dealer and was prepared to reveal a hidden stash.

Bott was most cooperative. She admitted tableting at Penlleinau. Her involvement, she said, wasn't financial. She felt that it was her contribution to society and that cannabis and acid, if used properly, lifted the veil to reveal the truth. She believed that using acid would make the world a better place.

'You begin to appreciate everything around you,' she said. 'The trees, stones, everything becomes beautiful. It really helps you to see the truth.'

Meanwhile, Munro admitted manufacturing acid at Seymour Road in 1976 and 1977. Cuthbertson admitted to being Todd's tableter and distributor for some four years. Lochhead and McDonnell not only admitted their drug deals but also implicated two others. At Brecon, a David Robertson admitted supplying acid bought from Hughes, and his dealing in Moroccan cannabis implicated Buzz Healey, who had been storing the stash for Hughes. Tcharney admitted supplying Solomon at his country retreat at Calmsden. There, he used a hole in a dry wall as a dead letter box to hide the tablets. His informer who phoned him from Esgairwen revealing Tcharney's arrest had been none other than the elusive Arnaboldi, who had once again given the police the slip.

Fielding was the next to cooperate. He led officers to Caesar's Camp at Nine Mile Ride and revealed a buried sandwich box which held two resealed boxes of Winalot dog food. Inside each of these were fifty small bags containing a total of over 100,000 acid tablets, more than had been seized worldwide in 1975.

On 28 March, the prisoners appeared in court next door to the police station. Over 30 of those arrested had now been released, most on police bail. The rest were remanded in custody. The interviews then continued with Todd refusing to cooperate to any degree. Kemp, however, was surprisingly open. He named firms he had used to buy equipment and chemicals. He revealed that the deposit box in Christine Bott's name at the Kantonal Bank in Zurich contained another key to a second box containing around two kilos of ergotamine tartrate. As for money, he revealed that there was around £50,000 deposited there. He denied having any money himself.

Tcharney had also been forthcoming, leading to the discovery of 50,000 tablets hidden under a stone in one of the fields at Esgairwen. These were half of a shipment of 100,000 tablets taken to Solomon but returned because the colour was not right.

More money was recovered from flats and rooms

in London connected with Annable and Cuthbertson. Such was the volume of information that four extra staff had to be brought in to follow up names, addresses and numbers. It would take them five months, working ten hours a day, five days a week.

Cuthbertson then offered a deal. If his wife was released from police bail, he would reveal a stash of LSD in Pangbourne Wood in the Reading area. Despite Cuthbertson travelling with them, the spot where the stash had been hidden could not be found.

Returning with him the following day, officers again drew a blank. Cuthbertson, desperate for the release of his wife, sought Todd's help. Todd promised to do so provided he wasn't compromised in any way. He travelled with Cuthbertson and the accompanying officers. With his help, and using a bulldozer, they found a black plastic bag containing three black, cylindrical containers. On examining the containers back at the Scene of Crime Department, one was found to contain nine plastic bags with 25 smaller bags inside. Each contained 1,008 dots or domes. This meant over 250,000 tablets in one canister. The second contained the same amount and the third slightly less. The total value was £800,000.

Meanwhile, Christine Bott offered to reveal where a stash of pure LSD and moulds had been buried in her garden. Under a compost heap in a corner of a potato patch, officers uncovered two brown bottles containing 120 grams of crystals, enough to produce 1,200,000 tablets worth some £1,500,000. Also recovered were 30 moulds and small perforated plastic boards used for tableting, identical to some of those found at Seymour Road. Wooden staging found there corresponded to the ones seen earlier at Plas Llysyn

She then proffered the information that equipment used at Plas Llysyn during the last run had been disposed of down a disused well. Four police officers immediately commandeered a mechanical digger from neighbour Huw Thomas' farm. The well was excavated and, indeed, pieces of smashed-up equipment and drums were discovered. One drum was identical to the two found previously in the cellar.

Bott also authorised officers to inspect her safety deposit box at the Kantonal Bank. There they found share certificates, stocks and bonds as well as money. It all totalled some £60,000, ten thousand pounds more than Kemp's estimate. Also found was the second key.

A third box was found, but could not be opened. The officers were elated when they were told that this box was owned jointly by Bott and Henry Barclay Todd. When Kemp was questioned about this, he blamed Thomas for destroying everything. He added that Thomas was a now a dead man, intimating that there was a contract out on him. Todd would not comment when questioned about the third box.

On April Fools' Day the remaining 31 prisoners were formally charged. Police would be limited in their questioning. They would have to restrict themselves to matters involving the recovery of stolen or dangerous property or to clear up ambiguities in previous statements.

The raided properties were still being guarded to protect any remaining evidence. A uniformed officer keeping watch on Penlleinau was handed a letter by the local postman. It had a Majorcan postmark and was addressed to Kemp and Bott. It was unsigned but had obviously been sent by Arnaboldi.

In the letter he regretted the recent falling-out. He was anxious to sort out the transfer of bonds and money, going into details of Kemp's holdings. He suggested a meeting with Bott, who would transfer $20,000 worth of bonds for cash. The letter revealed that Kemp owned $14,000 in bonds somewhere in Britain, but these were never found.

It became obvious that the falling-out had been over Arnaboldi's request that Kemp turn the share of the acid the American had received in Carno into tablet form. Kemp had refused.

Spanish police managed to find Arnaboldi in Deia and he was arrested. After holding him for three days, they had no choice other than to release him as there was no extradition treaty involving drugs offenders between Britain and Spain. He flew to New York where he was again held and released because it would take weeks to draw up an extradition request. He flew on to Tampa, Florida.

The jigsaw, however, was almost complete and the police realised that throughout the operation they had been tracking not one, but two LSD rings. Both had been operating simultaneously but had been unaware of each other.

The principal figure was undoubtedly Richard Kemp. In *Albion Dreaming* Andy Roberts traces the conspiracy that led to the formation of Operation Julie back to 1968, when David Solomon – having arrived in Cambridge the previous year with his wife and two daughters – met Kemp. Already living with Christine Bott, he was employed as a researcher at Liverpool University.

At the time, Solomon was attempting to synthesise THC, the active constituent of marijuana. Kemp helped him. Sometime in 1969 they decided to produce LSD, initially to finance the THC project. Arnaboldi supplied Kemp with 40 grams of ergotamine maleate. Kemp soon produced three weak batches of LSD at his Liverpool flat. He accidentally ingested a large amount – he had already taken a small amount – and was soon on 'a trip of cosmic proportions'. This was the moment when he changed from being a formal academic researcher to a believer.

This is when Ronald Stark seems to have joined in with what was to become the Welsh connection. It was Solomon who introduced him to Kemp, and it was Stark that recruited him to work on the THC project in a French laboratory in Paris. While doing so, Kemp stumbled on a method of producing almost pure LSD using a short-cut procedure. Later they moved the operation to Orléans. But Kemp then split with Stark and returned home. By 1972 he was producing LSD in various London flats, with Solomon financing the purchasing of the necessary chemicals. He then passed the LSD to Brian Cuthbertson for tableting, receiving in exchange £200 per gram. During one production run he manufactured 500 grams, thus earning himself

£100,000. His method was to produce a run, pack all the equipment away and then start again in another flat.

The tableted acid was then passed on to Henry Todd in the Reading area. The distribution chain included Russell Spenceley and Alston Hughes. Then came a disagreement between Kemp and Todd. Kemp always insisted on producing the purest acid possible. The purity of his acid was, apparently, 99.07 per cent. But his suspicions that his product was being diluted by Todd led him to buying some of his own drugs at a festival. When Cuthbertson tested it later, Kemp was horrified to discover that it was only half strength. This led to a parting of the ways.

This happened around late 1973. Apart from differences of opinion, Kemp now realised that he 'was the goose that laid the golden egg'. He was the man who could call the tune. But Todd's final outrage, according to Andy Roberts in *Albion Dreaming*, was to invest in General Franco's Spanish highway bonds.

Tendler and May in *The Brotherhood of Eternal Love* described Kemp's decision to make a break and move to Wales being partly due to his outlook and the way it differed from Todd's aspirations:

'To the chemist's way of thinking, Todd was nothing more than a dilettante whose values were mainly mercenary. As far as Todd was concerned, Kemp was difficult, arrogant and naïve ... The simmering differences came to a head with negotiations on future production ... It was almost an action replay of his split with Stark.'

Tendler and May, however, also suggest that the

split might have been motivated by mutual safety as much as by mutual dislike. It could have been a way of confusing the police.

Whatever the reason, Kemp was reconciled with Solomon and Arnaboldi. But he left London and sought a quiet place in Wales. With Arnaboldi, they toured in a caravan towed by Kemp's red Land Rover. Their meanderings led them to Plas Llysyn in Carno, the eighteenth-century mansion bought by Arnaboldi in June 1974. The £26,000 deal was largely financed by Arnaboldi selling his shares for £17,500. Kemp made up the difference.

Although Bott thought it to be 'a monstrous place', Kemp immediately set about installing a laboratory. He later bought Penlleinau, fifty miles to the south west near Tregaron. The fatal accident involving Kemp put paid to any production for most of 1975 and delayed it for nine months.

Todd, on the other hand, had recruited chemist Andy Munro to produce acid in a laboratory that was never located. They then moved to Seymour Road. Production there preceded Kemp's laboratory production by several months. From 1976 on, there were two laboratories in production.

By the spring of 1976, Kemp had completed the biggest production run of his career. He had converted seven kilos of ergotamine tartrate into 1,800 grams of LSD, enough to make nine million microdots. His work-rate was phenomenal, as noted by Tendler and May. Striving for increased yields and high quality, he managed to raise the yields by up to 25 and 30 per cent 'while only a sense of scientific modesty forbade him from claiming the LSD was 100 per cent pure'.

They continue: 'While others might take weeks, Kemp broke down the ergotamine in ten days; he took another two weeks to convert it into crystals he claimed would stay intact for hundreds of years. It meant working long, hard hours non-stop. The first stage of the process took twenty-four hours without a break, and after that the chemist slept for another twelve. As he worked, the air was full of fumes and particles so he was continually affected by the drug. Kemp worked out a system which allowed him to stagger production, so that while one operation was taking place he could switch attention to a material which had already passed through that stage. In between operations, Christine Bott would rescue him and take him back to the cottage for a rest.'

He then began tableting at the cottage using home-made equipment and was able to run off 50,000 in three hours. By the spring of 1977 it is estimated that he had passed on over 180,000 microdots to Tcharney to sell on to Solomon, who would pay $5,000 per 1,000 microdots. Kemp's dream of producing acid by the hundredweight was nearing reality.

Before the bust, police were unaware that Todd and Kemp had long worked together before their fierce quarrel made Kemp leave and strike out on his own. They were complete opposites. Kemp's motive was totally idealistic. He believed in the mantra 'turn on, tune in, drop out'. Todd was only interested in making money. So when he had taken to diluting their LSD and thus producing more but weaker acid, Kemp was incandescent. His ambition had been to produce the best and purest LSD ever made. So he left with Bott for Carno where he set up his own laboratory and realised his ambition.

Police now knew the structure of the London links. London-produced LSD was sold by Fielding to Richard Burden in London who in turn sold internationally. Among his customers was the Israeli Izchak, known as Zahi. Burden was the mysterious figure described by Spenceley as 'the other man'. He was known to have used the Last Resort restaurant as a base.

Fielding also supplied Russell Spenceley in Maesycrugiau. Spenceley sold on to Hughes at Llanddewi Brefi for £170 per thousand. Spenceley was believed to have sold him around 850,000 doses. Smiles sold on again for £200 per thousand to Tony Dalton in London, John Preece in Birmingham and Lochhead and McDonnell in Swindon. It was then sold on the street for £1 per tablet.

The Welsh ring was far simpler and more direct. Acid made at Plas Llysyn was sold to Tcharney who sold on to Solomon, mostly for worldwide export. Involved in that venture again was the Israeli Zahi. He was the only main player to be involved with both rings. Tcharney was estimated to have sold on around 200,000 tablets worth around £16,000. He had also supplied Solomon with some 182,000 tablets bound for Amsterdam and the States. Then there were the 50,000 discovered at Esgairwen.

Had Hughes only realized, he could have cut out the middle men by buying much purer LSD made by a brilliant biochemist living just up the road in Tregaron. Hughes' driver, Paul Healey, told me that neither he nor Hughes was aware of the Carno connection or the fact that the acid was being tableted only six miles away. In fact, neither of them knew of the existence of Kemp and Bott.

12

LOOSE ENDS

THE TRIAL WAS TO open on 12 January 1978 and would last three months. But with the trial just nine months away, police had still not completed the picture. Indeed, they never would. Still missing was much of Kemp's equipment and around 1.5 kilos of acid crystal, enough to produce 15,000,000 microdots worth some £75,000,000. Also missing were around 2,000,000 microdots produced during the last run at Seymour Road.

Lee seriously considered demolishing Penlleinau stone by stone and digging up the garden. It would cost up to £9,000 to rebuild the cottage but Lee believed that it would still make economic sense. He did not think, however, that he would be forced to take such drastic measures. Knowing the depth of the pair's love for the cottage, he believed that the threat in itself would be enough to loosen their tongues.

But Kemp insisted that the police had recovered everything. He admitted that he had been involved in tableting at his home and also that it had been a foolish act in view of Gerald Thomas' threat to inform on him. Lee wondered how Kemp had known of Thomas' threat.

Such was the extent of the operation that space

was at a premium. At Bristol's Horfield Prison, Healey remembered a whole floor being cleared to accommodate him and his fellow prisoners. For the administrative work, Swindon Police Station was too small so the team was given the additional use of a small police station in the town. As most officers had now returned to their various forces, staff were also at a premium. This resulted in a reshuffle with Harry Hull, Assistant Chief Constable of Wiltshire being made executive officer in charge of policy, Dennis Greenslade promoted to operational commander and Dick Lee promoted to detective chief inspector. Dai Rees and Ray Shipway were promoted to inspectors to help Lee while ten officers were drafted in.

The high number of prisoners to be dealt with and the volume of evidence almost overwhelmed the officers involved. Not only were the cells full and prisoners being locked up in all other available rooms but evidence and exhibits were also clogging up the gymnasium in five-foot-high heaps. Even the changing rooms and showers were full of documents, laboratory equipment and chemicals. All these had to be collated by a staff of only six officers.

Unexpectedly, a rapport was developing between the prisoners and their interrogators, as Andy Roberts states in *Albion Dreaming*: 'A peculiar bond quickly arose between the Operation Julie police officers and those they had arrested. The prisoners at first were refused the services of solicitors and had their clothes taken away for forensic examination. They were reduced to wearing blankets for warmth and modesty. Several police officers took pity on them and brought in their own clothes for the prisoners. Food also was brought in for those who were vegetarians.

'Dick Lee was aware of this and the erosion of professional boundaries worried him. In time, he called a meeting at which he reminded his officers their relationship with the prisoners should show respect for their humanity but should not extend to acts of personal kindness.'

With committal proceedings scheduled for June, there arose another problem. Red tape had slowed investigations in Switzerland to a standstill. There were even suggestions from above that banking inquiries in Switzerland should be abandoned.

In the meantime, Home Office research chemists reported that Kemp's acid was the purest ever known and that his formula was unique. As a result, Kemp's LSD was easily recognizable. As Lee commented, it was as good as a fingerprint.

Around this time the Italian police released their file on Stark. It included formulae for the synthesization of THC and LSD. The formula for acid was identical to Kemp's. It was also noted that Kemp, in 1972, was living less than a quarter of a mile from Stark. Yet Kemp had consistently denied being involved with Stark after 1970.

Police also discovered an informant, a girl who had been part of the Cambridge scene in the late sixties and the early seventies. She maintained that there had been a British connection with the Brotherhood of Eternal Love. She also remembered Solomon being supplied with impure LSD by an inorganic chemist known as Dick. Solomon was friendly with Stark as well as being close to Timothy Leary. It was Solomon who had introduced Stark to Dick, who then worked for Stark in France with the LSD crystals produced smuggled to America. She also revealed that Gerald Thomas had been visiting Britain prior to 1971.

For the loss of his chemist, Solomon was compensated with 0.25 kilos of pure acid crystal, enough for 2,500,000 tablets at a value of £1,250,000. Todd then arrived on the scene and helped Solomon convert the crystal into tablet form.

The informant went on to reveal a German connection and named the company that had supplied Kemp and Stark. She also dropped various names including Charles Druce, Arnaboldi and Tcharney. She added that after the French operation was closed down, Kemp moved to Cambridge and then to Bristol.

The girl's evidence, however, could not be used in court as the director of public prosecutions ruled that she had been too involved. This must have frustrated Lee as he was desperate to prove a connection between Kemp and the Brotherhood.

Attention then turned to the safety deposit boxes owned by some of those in custody. Attempts were made to access boxes belonging to Cuthbertson and Bott in the Kantonal bank in Zurich. In Cuthbertson's case, the person who attempted to access his box was a known criminal with a record for violence, theft and bank robbery. He produced a letter of authority fraudulently signed. He was apprehended and then expelled from Switzerland.

In Bott's case, a woman calling herself Laura Smart presented a certificate signed by Christine. Because an official hold had been issued on all boxes belonging to those arrested she was refused access. Bott admitted having signed a blank letter on Arnaboldi's request. She had done so in case she and Kemp needed money in an emergency, and trusted Arnaboldi with it. Laura Smart was an Englishwoman with a San Francisco address who had been working as a journalist.

Gradually, the boxes yielded their secrets. Bott's remaining box, under Kemp's name, was found to contain 1.2 kilos of ergotamine tartrate. In an account at the Votobel Bank, Todd had 10,637 in money and 983,311 in securities, all in Swiss francs. His boxes at the Kantonal Bank contained purchasing documents for ergotamine tartrate. His assets totalled £400,000.

Cuthbertson's account at the Votobel Bank contained 1,712 in Swiss francs and 415,150 in securities. In the Kantonal Bank he was found to have sequestered a one-kilo ingot of pure gold, 25 gold Krugerrands and 6,000 deutschmarks, worth a total of £200,000.

Solomon's boxes contained only small amounts, while a box jointly owned by Todd and Kemp was found to contain nothing but a newspaper cutting from *The Times* published in May 1975 showing a photograph of actor Ben Gazzara in the role of an American gangster. Lee was struck by his likeness to Stark.

Cuthbertson's boxes in banks in Périgueux

contained only relatively small amounts of money. Of Todd's known valuable stamp collection, no trace was found. Access to a bank deposit box and account in his name in Barbados was refused.

Stark's name had appeared so often that Lee requested that he be allowed to interview him in prison in Italy. His request was firmly refused. He was told in no uncertain manner to confine his enquiries to those already in custody. He did manage, however, to gain cooperation from the DEA, who sent over an agent to work with the Julie team for a few weeks.

Meanwhile, the 31 remaining prisoners were sent for trial at Bristol Crown Court. It was only then that Christine Bott, much to Dick Lee's relief, confessed to the officer assigned to her that Esgairwen would have been the next laboratory. His instincts had been correct all along.

Lee, however, was still not satisfied with his picture of Kemp. The cash recovered did not come near to what he should have earned during the seven years he had been involved in manufacturing. He also refused to accept Kemp's assertion that he was the one running his own LSD team. There were glaring gaps in accounts by others arrested. And he still pushed the need for a national drugs squad. In fact, since February 1976 Operation Julie had been just that in all but name. But senior officers were content to disband the squad and create another if and when an occasion demanded.

By late summer 1977 most members of the Julie team, including Lee himself, were returned to their forces. Some felt betrayed. In effect, as Lee and Pratt state in their book, they found that all their work and the experience gained was not considered to be of any value by the chief constables. So Lee and five of his men resigned in frustration. The five were Martyn Pritchard (Thames Valley), Johnny McWalter (West Midlands), Paul Durnell (Dorset and Bournemouth), Allen Buxton (West Midlands, who was also Georgie Fame's ex-drummer) and Eric Wright (Avon and Somerset, one of the pair of undercover cops who had been keeping tabs on Hughes at Llanddewi Brefi). Lee became a private investigator. Pritchard became a pub landlord.

In October 1977 came a breakthrough that would lead to the last significant discovery. A prisoner from among those arrested, whose name has never been disclosed, made a plea bargain. He was prepared to reveal the location of two kilos of crystal hidden by Kemp. The Home Secretary gave the nod and the anonymous informer told John Locke, who was appointed to lead the negotiations, to look under the floor tiles of Kemp and Bott's kitchen. Greenslade, Rees and Shipway were joined at the cottage by Richie Parry, Noir Bowen and others on 1 December. About a foot below the level of the floor they uncovered a plastic box. It was sent unopened directly to the police laboratory at Aldermaston. It revealed 1.3 kilos of acid crystals, enough for 13,000,000 doses worth £65,000,000. It was the greatest stash of drugs discovered anywhere in the world.

The betrayal infuriated Kemp, so much so that he sat down and wrote a 53-page statement detailing his part in the production of acid since 1968. This was when he first met Solomon through a mutual college classmate. It was a year later when Solomon suggested that he should produce LSD. This he did at his Liverpool home, where he lived with his parents.

He then met Paul Arnaboldi, who supplied him with ergotamine tartrate. The method he used, hiding it in a hollowed-out magazine, was exactly the same method used by Gerald Thomas.

Kemp duly converted the raw material into liquid LSD. But it was of a poor quality. This was smuggled to Canada. The smuggler was Thomas, although Kemp did not mention that fact.

Later that summer he first produced his own acid and accidentally ingested a large dose. He swore he would never again work alone in an LSD laboratory. Solomon invited him to his home in Cambridge to meet Ronald Stark, who invited Kemp to work for him. He dropped out from college in January 1970 and moved to Paris where he worked in Stark's laboratory within a larger legitimate laboratory. Kemp produced a shipment of a kilo destined for America. This was when he discovered the method of producing almost pure acid.

In May he visited Switzerland with Stark where he met two members of the Brotherhood, though he denied knowing who they were at the time. Lee dismissed his denial. Owning up to knowing members of the Brotherhood would have extended the operation from being a British-based inquiry into a global inquiry.

Kemp returned to Paris but became disillusioned

with Stark and travelled back to England where he met Solomon and Todd in Cambridge. The two were now tableting Stark's LSD while Todd was marketing as well. Solomon was given 0.25 kilos of crystal by Stark, presumably as a reward for the introduction of his brilliant chemist.

Kemp then moved to London where he made more LSD. This was when he broke completely with Stark. He then went back to Liverpool where he produced 250 grams of acid.

This was a crucial time in the story, when Munro arrived on the scene and was asked by Kemp to analyse the contents of Todd's tablets. The analysis confirmed what Kemp had suspected. The tablets had been halved in strength from 200 micrograms to 100 micrograms. He also accused Todd of stealing £7,000 from him. Kemp asked Thomas to replace Todd as a tableter. But Thomas tried to cheat on him as well. This was just before Thomas was arrested in Canada, when the Brotherhood was busted and when Leary was arrested in Afghanistan.

Kemp denied any contact with Thomas after that. In 1973, when Thomas threatened to inform on the gang, Kemp moved out of London and looked for a suitable laboratory, eventually settling for Plas Llysyn. Todd had moved out of London to set up a lab in Cambridge before moving back to the capital. But Lee was not convinced about the split between Kemp and Todd. If it had been final, why did they still have a joint safe deposit box in Zurich?

Kemp said that he had spent late 1974 renovating Plas Llysyn. Arnaboldi came over in January 1975 to help with the work of setting up the laboratory. Their hopes of commencing production in April were dashed by the fatal accident involving Kemp. Meanwhile, Stark was arrested in Italy at the beginning of that year and was found to be in possession of a copy of Kemp's synthesis. And if Petroff was the second American seen at the mansion in 1976, this again suggested a Brotherhood connection.

Kemp ended his statement stating: 'I would like to add that my present circumstances are as follows. I have no hidden stash of LSD or money. I have no secret bank account in any foreign country. I have no valuable assets, such as jewellery, coins or stamps. I own no property nor even a motor car. My total worldly possessions are the £12 I have in the canteen account at Horfield Prison. When I am released from prison I'll have nothing to come out to whatever.'

Unlike himself, said Kemp, a fellow prisoner was still receiving cash from abroad emanating from the sale of LSD made by Kemp. This man, he added, was to receive £50,000 from his last sale, £7,000 of which he had already received.

Kemp had always maintained that the trial was political rather than criminal. Writing to a friend from prison, he said, 'We have been hunted down, not because of a few bad trips or LSD-associated deaths, but because of the dramatic political effect we have been having.'

In another letter he wrote, 'We were really very small potatoes in a world context. My estimate of our total LSD contribution over the complete period of our activity was one and a half.' Compare this to

Dennis Greenslade's boast after the trial that Kemp and the others had been responsible for producing 60 per cent of the world's supply of LSD.

13

THE FINAL CURTAIN

MR JUSTICE PARK PRESIDED over the hearings at Bristol Crown Court which opened on 12 January 1978. Such was the demand for seats in the public gallery that for the first time in the history of criminal trials in the city, tickets had to be allocated.

Dick Lee was not happy with the venue. He believed that such a high profile hearing deserved the Old Bailey, thus ensuring the highest possible publicity.

Justice Park decided to sentence the guilty prisoners in two batches. He wanted to clear the decks of the minor players, so he sentenced them first.

David John Heasman, a friend of Todd, had not been a part of the main conspiracy. But the large stash of cannabis discovered in his flat earned him two years in jail.

Paul 'Buzz' Healey (28) was also innocent of any conspiracy charges. He had been Alston Hughes' driver, and the 10 pounds of Moroccan cannabis found in his possession earned him a one-year sentence. The stash belonged to Hughes, who was found guilty of being involved in the Moroccan cannabis conspiracy. His sentence was postponed till the completion of the second hearing.

Other members of the Moroccan cannabis

smuggling ring that had supplied Hughes and were apprehended during Operation Julie inquiries were the next to go down. They had used a caravan fitted with false compartments to make two trips to Morocco. Hughes had contributed £2,000 towards the venture. The sentences were: David Robertson of Gelli Gellogas, Llanddewi near Brecon and Nicholas Pelopida, Einon Farm, Builth Wells – four years; Christopher Osborne, Llwyncelyn, Merthyr Cynog, Brecon and Gordon Evans, Victoria Road, Ebbw Vale – two years; Christopher Casa-Grande, St Dials, Cwmbran and Mostyn Crewe, Ann's Court, Gwaun Helyg, Ebbw Vale – one year.

Four defendants found guilty of an LSD conspiracy were sentenced to a total of 18 years, with William Lochhead and John McDonnell receiving eight years each and Philip Hemmings and Paul Geros one year each.

John Lindsey Preece was sentenced to four years for supplying LSD and other drugs in the Birmingham area.

Then came Kemp's final indignity. Another unnamed prisoner, eager to gain a favour when his sentencing came around, informed the authorities that Kemp had £16,000 hidden for his release. Originally hidden in Bott's Renault, it had been moved and hidden under stones on the bank of a stream at Esgairwen.

The informer did not know that the money had, in the meantime, been moved again further up the stream. Police almost gave up the search when Noir Bowen and Vince Castle came up trumps. Bowen instinctively pulled back a bunch of reeds and there, underneath the bank in a black plastic bag, was the hidden cash. But it did not amount to the £16,000 the informer had detailed. There was only £11,000. Poor Kemp had been robbed of £5,000 by one of his own people.

Most of the main players had pleaded guilty to conspiracy to manufacture and distribute LSD before the hearing at Bristol's second court. Of the principal conspirators, only Bott, Cuthbertson and Spenceley had pleaded not guilty. The judge added to the tension by delaying his entrance before the sentencing. He then began by emphasising the large profits made from manufacturing and dealing in LSD and the difficulty in detecting such activities. 'Indeed, it takes an operation on the scale of Operation Julie to stop or even curtail those drug deals,' he said.

He then went on to express his regret that one consequence was that severe sentencing should be passed 'on people with excellent characters, some with excellent professional qualifications'.

He proceeded to sentence the 17 defendants to a total of 124 years. The breakdown was: Kemp (34), the principal player, and Todd (32), his former partner – 13 years each; Brian Cuthbertson (29), the go-between in the supply network – 11 years; Solomon (52), Munro (29) and Spenceley (28) – 10 years each; Bott (32) – nine years; Fielding (29) and Hughes (30) – eight years each. As for the others, David Todd, Annable and Burden were given six years; Dalton, five years; Mark Tcharney, three years, and Douglas Flanagan, Janine Spenceley and Monica Kenyon, Dalton's girlfriend, two years suspended. The total sentencing for the trial amounted to 170 years.

Kemp had expected the then maximum of 14 years. Bott, on the other hand, seemed to have been treated extremely harshly. She was basically a decent, caring woman who believed in what she and Kemp were doing. That in itself is no mitigation, but unlike most of the principals, money was not a motive in her case. She was involved, yes, but so were wives or girlfriends of some of the others. Yet those other wives or partners found guilty had their sentences suspended. As Munro ruefully commented, 'Bott got nine years for making sandwiches. I got ten years for making acid.'

There was an obvious anomaly in the sentencing. Janine Spenceley, for instance, had admitted dealing in LSD on her husband's request. She only received a suspended sentence. Bott's mistake was probably to be too honest in stating and arguing her belief in the benefits of taking LSD under controlled conditions.

In *Albion Dreaming*, Andy Robert comments: 'Had Bott put spin on her testimony, played the vulnerable female and claimed that Kemp had coerced her into a life of illicit LSD manufacture, the chances are she would have walked free from the court with a suspended sentence at most.'

All those sentenced have long been released. Most have disappeared. I have not attempted to trace any of them. They have served their sentences and deserve their privacy. Others have tried to track some of them down. I will not go into details here for the reason given, but it seems that their arrest and resulting trial drove Kemp and Bott apart after their release. Kemp has, apparently, been seen in Goa and Bott is said to have settled in the south west of Ireland. No-one really knows.

Stark died in 1982 and Solomon in April 2007. Munro disappeared completely, but is believed to have cooperated with a journalist. Hughes has been seen in a London pub, his dazzling smile as bright as ever. Spenceley stayed in west Wales and Tcharney, an excellent doctor, also returned to work in the area. In fact, he agreed to an interview with a *Cambrian News* reporter, Arthur Williams, but refused to have his photograph taken.

Tcharney was released three years after his arrest. He had been struck off the medical register following his conviction. But an Aberystwyth GP, Dr D Rowland Edwards, who was aware of his conviction, invited him to join his practice and he was reinstated by a General Medical Council committee following his release from prison.

'I always got on well with people in the Lampeter area when I was a locum at Llanybydder previously, and I was very happy when Dr Edwards offered me the job,' he told the reporter. He added that he had applied for several jobs in Wales as he loved the country and its people. He intended to work with Dr Edwards for a year and had no definite plans for the future, although he had an interest in psychiatry.

He regretted the publicity, however, as it complicated any relationship with his patients. 'I appeared before a disciplinary committee in July and it was decided that I was fit to be included on the medical register,' he said.

'As far as I am concerned, that should be sufficient guarantee to any patient that I am considered to be a reliable person.' He revealed that he had decided to drop the 'T' in his surname and would henceforth be known as Mark Charney in order to protect his identity.

Todd served seven and a half years and turned upon his release to one of his great loves – mountaineering. He started a business supplying oxygen cylinders to climbers. He was involved in a private prosecution following the death of a climber who experienced problems with his oxygen supply. He was cleared of any blame.

The only one involved who returned and lived quite openly was Paul Healey, Alston Hughes' driver. Healey returned to Llanddewi Brefi, working as a builder before taking over a pub near Lampeter. Ironically it stood just across the road from the Ram Inn, scene of the infamous switch between Spenceley and Hughes, when Healey himself was present. He is a likeable character who, to his eternal credit, has refused to cash in on his knowledge of the acid conspiracy. He was not directly involved in it, but as Hughes' driver there is a lot that he does know. He now works as a builder.

After he was arrested in 1977 he was allowed bail on a surety of £20,000, a sum that he could never have raised. Immediately, a Tregaron businessman put up the money and he was released. The businessman's faith in Healey conforming to bail conditions was justified.

Two days after the sentencing, the judge ordered

the forfeiture of the prisoners' British assets. He could not make such an order for assets discovered abroad. The Swiss authorities had already indicated that any assets discovered would be seized. It was intended that the value of all assets seized, around £1 million, should be put into a public fund that would then cover the cost of Operation Julie. The total cost was originally said to be £2 million, but was then lowered to around £500,000.

Later, the forfeiture was overturned on appeal at the House of Lords, a decision that was announced 'with considerable regret' by Lord Diplock. An appeal against the order for the forfeiture of money, bonds and property had been made by Brian Cuthbertson and Henry Todd. This was allowed as their offences did not fall within the remit of the 1971 Act.

The relief for those affected was not long lasting, however. The Inland Revenue stepped in and soon relieved them of most of their assets.

14

A DOCTOR WRITES

RICHARD KEMP'S INTENTION IN writing his 53-page testimony was to present it as his defence in court. But he was persuaded not to by his lawyer, as it could lead the judge to pass a heavier sentence. He did, however, pass his 8,000-word statement on to *Cambrian News* journalist Patrick O'Brien who duly published the gist of the confession in the paper on Friday 17 March, a week following the sentencing. The article was headed: 'Microdoctrine – the beliefs behind Kemp's LSD.'

This was, undoubtedly, Kemp's philosophical credo. In it he stated that he believed society would have to change rapidly if ecological disaster and social chaos were to be avoided. 'In common with some expert scientific opinion he was convinced that, if Earth's raw materials were to be conserved and pollution reduced to a tolerable level, there would be a revolution in people's attitude,' wrote O'Brien. 'And he believed LSD could spark changes in outlook which would put the world on the road to survival.'

He then quoted Kemp: 'I do have deeply-held convictions as to the possible aspects of the use of LSD. It was these that provided the motivation for engaging in the activities for which I am before your Lordship, and NOT the desire to make money by means of a criminal activity.'

He had prepared the hand-written document, said O'Brien, in order that his views would emerge clearly and because 'the crazy exaggerations' of much media reporting had 'really got me down no end'.

Kemp continued, 'I am particularly anxious to counter the impression that I am an evil man so bound up in greed that I was uncaring or unmindful of the possible harmful effects resulting from what I did.

'I am not trying to ignore or excuse the fact that I have broken the law. I wish only to put the crime in perspective in which I see it.'

O'Brien explained that on ecology and conservation, Kemp believed that it was obvious that we were living on the world's capital rather than its income. To achieve a level of consumption that was reasonable, taking into account the Earth's limited and dwindling resources, two things would be necessary: 'People will have to accept a lower standard of living by becoming content with having things which are necessary for survival, and luxuries will have to be kept to a minimum.

'Secondly, those goods which are supplied will have to be built to have the longest possible lifespan, at the end of which they must be capable of being recycled.'

Kemp added in the document, described as 'my LSD philosophy': 'Changes in policy by manufacturers will come about only if sufficient pressure for such change is generated by the public.

'In as far as LSD can catalyse such a change in

members of the public, it can contribute to this end.'

Kemp said that only if people found greater contentment within themselves and became free of outdated and trivial social status would they be able to accept the necessity of a life which revolved less around material things.

Kemp admitted to taking LSD over 200 times other than in the course of manufacture. He continued, 'It has been my experience, and that of many of those I know, that LSD helps one realise that happiness is a state of mind and not a state of ownership.'

But he made plain that he had not yet freed himself 'from the dependence on material things which we have encouraged to develop throughout our lives'. He did not claim that this freedom was 'an inevitable result of LSD experiences'.

Kemp continued, 'But I feel that I, and many of those I know, have started down the road to a greater reliance on our inner resources.

'Because of the realisation that contentment is a state of mind, one compensates less for unhappiness by buying things.

'This is why I feel that, if a large number of people were to experience this truth, whether by means of LSD or by means of an appropriate discipline, such as yoga or meditation, the problems resulting from consumerism would be to a large extent solved.'

O'Brien stated that Kemp practised what he preached on simple living. 'The £7,000 Blaencaron cottage he shared with Dr Christine Bott had few luxuries,' he said. There was no television or central heating, the sparse furnishings tended to be threadbare and the walls of the rooms were treated merely to an annual coating of white cement paint.

'A deep freeze stood in the lean-to but the *tŷ bach* (outside toilet) maintained its original role.

'The only ostentatious touch in the two-bedroomed home is a Victorian cast-iron spiral staircase, which Kemp bought in London and installed himself.

'They ate simply – an assortment of vegetables from the immaculately laid-out garden, milk, cheese and yoghurt from their two pedigree goats, eggs from their half-a-dozen hens.

'He was committed to organic (non-chemical) gardening and belonged to the West Wales Soil Association. During the 1976 drought, before sinking his own well with the help of a water diviner he spent hours daily lugging water by truck to his vegetable beds from a river half a mile away.'

Kemp claimed, said O'Brien, that a sharp awareness of the importance of conservation and ecology was just one example of how clear-sightedness through LSD could manifest itself. He believed the drug raised the barrier separating people from the unconscious part of their minds, and another benefit this could bring was to help to alleviate or eliminate everyday neurotic problems.

Kemp added that LSD was sometimes used as an end in itself because it enhanced all the senses with everything appearing more beautiful.

'When people first use LSD they tend to concentrate on this aspect of the experience,' wrote Kemp, 'but later they begin to use LSD as a means to learn about themselves, rather than as an end.'

He added, 'If it were just a question of satisfying people's pleasure – seeking desires – I would not have become involved. However, I believe that an end towards which LSD is a means is personally and socially beneficial. This is the way I, and most of the people I know, use it.

'I have never believed that LSD is the substitute for the hard work required to change oneself. One might say it is a signpost pointing a way to self-discovery.'

In his treatise he did not try to ignore the dangers of the drug. Anyone involved in the illegal supply of LSD, he wrote, was obviously running the risk of exposing certain people to negative experiences with which they could not cope, and to which they may develop a panic reaction.

He added, 'I must emphasise that in my experience of LSD use and my observation of other LSD users I have NEVER SEEN a person develop a reaction which has led to uncontrollable behaviour, aggressiveness or attempts to harm themselves or others.

'However, I do accept that this may have occurred, but I am quite certain that it only happens when LSD is used in circumstances far removed from those recommended by all concerned with the drug, and that such events are extremely rare. I would like to contrast myself with the heroin dealer who sells to others something which he knows is addictive and does no good and which therefore he doesn't take himself. Chronic dependence on LSD is almost unknown and no-one believes it is addictive.'

He stressed that children should be protected. And he accepted the fact that some of those under the age of majority may have been exposed to something whose nature and proper use they did not fully understand.

'I would certainly support a system of social control,' he wrote, 'including education about the nature and use of LSD, backed by laws, where appropriate, to protect those who are not fully able to take decisions for themselves, and to cover situations in which the use of LSD became a matter for public rather than private concern. One obvious example is driving a car on a public road.'

Kemp continued, 'The present climate of opinion and law effectively forced me to make a choice between making LSD available without social controls, with the small risk inherent in this approach, or not making it available at all.

'Believing as I did that the benefits are so widespread and so urgently necessary if we are to have any chance of solving the pressing problems of the modern world, I felt I had no choice but to adopt the course which has led me to the dock and your Lordship's judgement.'

He maintained that other drugs, particularly alcohol, amphetamines, opiates and tobacco were far more dangerous than LSD. Many would agree with him.

Detective Sergeant Dai Rees, however, promoted to Detective Inspector following the arrests, was totally convinced of the success of Operation Julie and of the righteousness of the decision to pursue the conspirators, as well as his part in the operation.

'Initially I was a Detective Sergeant with various

roles of investigating; surveillance on suspect individuals and premises,' he told BBC Wales on 22 February 2007. 'These duties resulted in long periods of isolation in outlandish places, and took to me all parts of the UK, and France. In France I had the privilege of working through the Paris Interpol Office, and the French Police Specialist Drugs team.

'Following promotion... my role changed to preparing evidence for the prosecution case, and liaison with the Director of Public Prosecutions, and the prosecution team at the Crown Court in Bristol.'

He then went on to make claims that Kemp and his co-defendants would certainly question: 'The unlawful use of LSD had resulted in many murders, aggravated assaults, suicides, and serious psychological disorders amongst those who used it. The knowledge that persons manufacturing LSD were making vast profits and the consequences of its use upon those taking it was a very high motivating factor for the Operation Julie team. The success of the operation was a severe setback to the criminal fraternity, but most importantly prevented loss of life and injury upon those who saw its use as a "social mind-bending experience".'

He also spoke of the hardship he and other officers suffered. 'The length of the investigation created many personal, social and domestic difficulties and the long periods spent away from our families the worst. Secrecy was paramount and the dire consequences of breaching that security was forcibly impressed on every member of the team.

'At the conclusion, some highly educated and

skilful people were imprisoned. My personal feelings at the conclusion were "has it been worth it"? I remain convinced on many aspects. However, some recent political decisions to reclassify some "drugs" is very disheartening. These decisions do little to help society in general, the well being of individuals, or the police service.

'I am heartened that Operation Julie was the forerunner to many subsequent and current successful investigations. Many lessons were learned. We would do well to bear that in mind and lend our support to the police officers who continue to commit themselves to the well being of our young people and society in general.'

Kemp and Rees' outlooks were miles apart and graphically reflect differing opinions on LSD and its effects.

15

FLASHBACK TIME

FOLLOWING THE SENTENCING ON Tuesday, 8 March 1978, the newspapers – especially the red tops – were sensational in their praise for Operation Julie. They heralded the smashing of the world's greatest drugs ring and blackened the characters of the perpetrators.

There is no doubt that Operation Julie, within its brief, was a great success. It did what it was set up to do – destroy LSD production in Britain. But it did not destroy the supply. Even before the trial began, LSD was flooding in from California. And there are many unanswered questions. Did Lee's fixation with identifying a global conspiracy harm, rather than help the inquiry? Proving it would have helped advance his goal of establishing a national drugs squad.

Despite Lee's almost obsessive quest to find a connection between Kemp and the Brotherhood, he failed. Proving that Kemp knew people who themselves knew prominent members of the Brotherhood was obviously not enough.

Lee made much of the argument that Kemp and Todd must have remained as partners after the supposed split, based on the fact that they did not dissolve their joint ownership of a bank deposit box.

However, when the box was opened, it contained nothing but a newspaper clipping. There could be a simple answer that Lee did not contemplate. Without any incriminating evidence or money in the box, would cancelling their arrangement have been worth the bother?

This is not to dispute Operation Julie's success. No-one can disagree with some of Justice Park's comments after the sentencing was over. He addressed 21 officers of the Julie team who were called to face him. Many of them wore a tie designed by Detective Constable Alun Morgan depicting eleven clasped hands, representing the eleven forces involved in the investigation. The hands encircled an ear of rye, from which ergotamine tartrate, the basis of acid, is obtained.

Mr Justice Park said, 'I can delay no longer the public expression of my admiration about Operation Julie. Over the last few days the press and the television have rightly given tremendous coverage to the amazing detective work which led to these arrests and to the extreme hardship endured by the many police officers involved in it... '

He went on to mention facts not referred to earlier in court: 'I refer to the long separation of officers from their families and the need for total secrecy about the reasons for those separations and the consequent misunderstandings and strain which I hear some family relationships underwent. And so, these police officers, and these police activities required of the police officers, are sacrifices of the kind which policemen and policewomen, along with other members of the public are expected to endure only in wartime, never in peacetime.'

He also referred to two aspects of Operation Julie that required special mention. One was the manner in which the officers were able to create a trust and understanding during interviews with those whom they arrested. Two officers who had arrested and interviewed defendants were called, during the pleas for mitigation, as witnesses for the defence.

Secondly, he drew attention to the fact that many of the defendants had spoken of the fairness with which they were treated. Indeed, only one police officer's evidence had been seriously challenged.

But some are still sceptical, none more so than John May on his website *The Generalist*, where he re-published an article he had contributed to the *New Musical Express* on 18 March 1978 under the name Dick Tracey. In it he was scathing in his reaction to the reporting of the operation and the consequent trial. His comments are well worth noting.

To May, it reflected the community and street feeling that 'the whole thing had been hyped up to fit authoritarian agendas through the mouthpiece of the national press'. He also criticized the 'savage sentencing'. Operation Julie, he said, provided the press with a field day, allowing them to dust off all the old clichés and trot them out in print.

May based his article on a statement made by one of the defence lawyers at the trial: 'Never in the history of British crime has the police public relations been so effective and so exaggerated. It has been accepted blindly and blithely by all concerned.'

He described the official version of Operation Julie as 'an incredible display of media hand-holding' and 'a comforting picture of police efficiency smashing an evil international drug network so that the school kids of our nation can be protected from the threat of that of "heaven-or-hell" drug LSD ... Simply put, the police offered the press their version of an exciting story, and they took it hook, line and sinker'.

May contended that the whole affair had a great deal to do with internal police politics, with the Julie team working outside the traditional police structures as an elite crew, and their activities forming the basis for Detective Chief Superintendent Greenslade's vision for a national drug squad.

'The team, characterised by the *Mirror* as "a handful of shabby supercops", were so secretive that, according to *The Times*, even the Metropolitan Police did not know of the planned raids until the last possible moment. But I find this to have been quite understandable as secrecy was at a premium. And there was little love lost between Lee and the Met, who had blocked him on every occasion.'

Nevertheless, May continued: 'The Julie squad used every available trick in the book to break the case.' At the farm in Wales they used for surveillance, 'tons of secret monitoring equipment and scrambler telephones' – some on loan from the Whitehall security services – were quietly installed. May was obviously unaware of another allegation – that Julie officers received the cooperation of even the US Air Force. Surveillance photographs of an open-air party at Tcharney's home at Esgairwen have apparently been seen. They were allegedly taken from an American F-111 military aircraft.

May added, 'Policemen masqueraded as hippies for months on end, infiltrated festivals, communes and the like in search of information.' Foremost among these, said May, was Detective Sergeant Martyn Pritchard, described by the *Mail* as 'more hippy than policeman'. Interestingly, the *Mirror*, who published Pritchard's own story, revealed that they had taken a picture of him when he had to give evidence after revealing a cannabis racket in 1975. He said, 'The *Daily Mirror* published a rear-view picture of me so that it wouldn't blow my cover.'

May continued: 'Even Detective Chief Inspector Lee, the operations expert from the Thames Valley Drug Squad, indulged in fancy dress, posing as "a London businessman recuperating from a major heart problem". The police's Maigret-like expertise has been widely praised but, according to one defence lawyer, it's a myth.'

According to the lawyer, added May, rather than getting information as a result of their own investigations, it was all handed to them on a plate. The main leads were provided by Ronald Stark, a former associate who shopped the others when busted for heroin in Italy.

He was also critical of Lee for not moving sooner against the lab at Plas Llysyn. According to the *Mail*, Lee had known of the existence of the acid factory in Carno for some time before the final raids, and also knew the drugs from there would be distributed throughout the world. He knew they would be taken by young people whose lives could be ruined – and if LSD was as dangerous as the police and Home Office alleged, they might even die as a result. He knew he could stop their sale by raiding the mansion, but he decided not to. The *Mail* presented this, not as a criticism but as a picture of Lee's heroic dilemma. Had it not been for Lee's delay, said May, Arnaboldi and the international dealer known as Zahi could well have been apprehended. But the delay gave them the opportunity to flee.

'Following their success, real or overstated, Greenslade and others began pushing their idea for a super-police unit – an FBI style national drug squad – who, they claimed, would be able to combat the drug menace more effectively. Many papers took their lead and made their own demands for such a force to be set up – notably the *Mirror* and the *Express*.'

May continued, 'Greenslade boasted: "The operation was successful beyond my wildest dreams. This could pave the way for a national police force." Presumably, also in his dreams, with Detective Chief Superintendent Greenslade at the helm.'

May questioned the amount of LSD produced. The *Mail* claimed 15 million doses; *The Times* 20-60 million, supplying a dozen countries. The *Mirror* claimed that in 1976 alone, the gang's turnover reached an estimated £200 million – equal to that of British Home Stores. This was disputed by a defence lawyer. He claimed that the total syndicate take was nearer £700,000 throughout their entire operations.

'Then there was the question of what fraction of the total LSD market the syndicate's output represented,' wrote May. 'The *Mirror* claimed it was "two-thirds of the world's supply", BBC News said 90 per cent of Britain's and 60 per cent of the world's supply, while Greenslade told the *Express*: "In our view 95 per cent of LSD in Britain was coming from this source and so was half the world's supply." Of course, these things are impossible to gauge, but the mere act of printing them renders them "official".

When it came to the street price, the estimates were even more diverse. The *Express* claimed that it was priced at £1 a tab when the syndicate was in operation but that, since the bust, the street price had shot up to £5 or even £8 a tab, a fact quoted in court. On the other hand, *The Times* said: "Last week in London it could be bought for £1 a dose or £40 a thousand."

The Release organisation, experts on drugs and drug law, confirmed largely what *The Times* had said. It revealed to the *New Musical Express* soon after the trial that the bulk price was then £40 for 4,000, or 10p a tab, with a street price of £1 a tab. Acid, said Release, was as easily obtainable as cannabis.

Most insidious of all, said May, was the *Express* story that stated: 'All too many young people have experimented with LSD for the thrill. One was 16-year-old June Duggan and it killed her.' Now for the punchline: 'It could not be proved that her pill came from the gang sentenced at Bristol, but in view of their huge output it seems possible.'

The police in turn, he said, were supported in their attitude by the trial judge, Mr Justice Park, who ignored the expert evidence of Dr Martin

Mitcheson who ran the University College Hospital drug dependence clinic. Mitcheson told the court that LSD, not being an addictive drug, carried 'relatively small risks compared to other dangerous drugs' and he claimed that any comparison to other drugs was irrelevant.

May, however, was in a minority. The *Express* and the *Mirror* released books on Operation Julie soon after the trial ended lauding it as an unqualified success. The early release of the books implies that the authors Dick Lee (with Colin Pratt of the *Express*) in the first instance and Martyn Pritchard (with Ed Laxton) in the second had been working closely with the two newspapers for some time. Indeed, Pritchard's memoirs were published by Mirror Books.

All the newspapers were united save for radical publications such as the *International Times*, *The Leveller* and the *New Musical Express*. The tabloids attempted to outdo one another with their lurid stories. There was talk of acid being produced to finance the Angry Brigade, the Red Brigade and the IRA. Most of all, though, the papers vied with each other in speculating on the sums of LSD and money reputed to have been made by the conspirators.

The *Mirror* in particular went to town with a heading that announced: 'We'll blow a million minds.' The story regurgitated a version the old, old story of contaminating a reservoir or lake with nuclear waste. This time it was to have been acid. It also went back to those scare stories in the US at the time of the Brotherhood. The reservoir to be targeted, probably chosen at random by the *Mirror*, was one of those in mid Wales supplying Birmingham. Christine Bott seemed to have identified the real motive of the media's fixation. She said: 'If I thought there was a crime, I thought it had more to do with making money than LSD.'

It should be noted that despite all the pre-trial references to terrorist connections deliberately leaked to certain newspapers, not one of the defendants was charged with anything relating to terrorism or of having even a remotely political motive.

Since Operation Julie there has been only one LSD trial of note in Britain. In 2004 police arrested Casey Hardison, an American living near Brighton. A laboratory was discovered at his home with 146,000 acid doses dropped onto blotters, as well as other drugs.

Hardison, a medical anthropologist and LSD activist, was alleged to have made £125,000 from his venture – peanuts compared to the proceeds of the Operation Julie conspiracy. He maintained that money wasn't his motive. It was rather ideological and he was a pioneer in the study of LSD. Indeed, he had published various papers on the subject. Any money accumulated would go towards further study. The judge ignored his claims. So, 36 years after Richard Kemp was jailed for 13 years, Hardison received seven years longer for his one-man operation that netted but a fraction of what Kemp and Todd's LSD rings accumulated.

During the late 1960s and the early 1970s, and during a slight surge at the end of the 1980s, LSD was adopted as the recreational drug of choice. It has since gradually decreased in popularity – not as a result of police prosecutions – but as a result of being overtaken by more popular drugs such as cocaine and ecstasy. So, despite Operation Julie's success, real or imagined, LSD would have died a natural death anyway.

16

BETWEEN THE LINES

HINDSIGHT, AS BILLY WILDER once said, is always twenty-twenty. And looking back on early 1967 makes me feel very foolish. There were signs that something was in the air, signs that I either didn't see or didn't appreciate. While Lucy was up there in the sky with diamonds, I was too busy looking at the ground. That I was not alone brings little comfort.

A few weeks before Operation Julie officers swooped, I was in the Talbot Hotel in Tregaron one afternoon chatting to one of the locals. We were discussing the recent influx of strangers into the area. He then confided in me saying that a complete stranger had approached him in the bar a few weeks previously, carrying a holdall. Out of the blue, after some small talk, he had been offered him a considerable sum of money for looking after the bag. However, afraid that the stranger might belong to the IRA or was perhaps a bank-robber, he declined.

Following the raids, locals were suddenly well-informed. Tongues began to wag. Oh, yes, they had known all along. Local van deliverymen had been involved, no questions asked, in ferrying suspect packages. One typical story tells of a local man asked to keep a package for one of the dealers involved. Following the swoop, the man opened the package and discovered some £11,000. So frightened was he that the money could be traced to him that he burnt the lot. Fact? Fiction? Who knows?

Les Lewis, manager of the Talbot admits to being completely duped by 'Mr Calvert'. There are many others, however, who swear that they had known all along that the convivial London businessman was an undercover cop. Locals suddenly maintained that they had been well aware all along that 'those two' (Kemp and Bott) had been up to no good. They were too quiet, weren't they? Not mixing. And they were English, weren't they?

Suddenly, everyone knew everyone that was involved, or at least knew of someone who knew them. Telling porkies to journalists became an industry. And many a reporter was conned out of his or her expense allowance through exchanging drinks as bribes for fictitious information.

Despite all this, the signs had been there. At the Foelallt and the New Inn in Llanddewi Brefi, Alston 'Smiles' Hughes had been spending as if there was no tomorrow. He would light cigarettes with five pound notes. At Christmas time he would hand out bottles of whiskey to old age pensioners. One lady was given a cut glass ornament for no apparent reason. How could he afford such generosity when he wasn't in regular work?

Hughes became a legend in the area. According to Owen Thomas of the Black Lion at Lampeter he would flash endless wads of money. He would put five or ten pound notes in charity boxes. And he had a taste for Champagne. One day at the Black Lion he is said to have supped six bottles of bubbly, leaving the empties in a line on the counter.

A typical story involved him playing cards late at night at the New Inn. One of the crew asked the time. Smiles was surprised that the enquirer did not own a watch. He immediately took off his own watch and handed it to him. By today, of course, the watch – a fairly ordinary make – has become a Rolex. Card schools would also be held at his home. His friends got used to seeing him using betting money kept in wads in cereal boxes.

He was one of a crew of locals who sometimes attended Chepstow Races. There, a horse called Cannabis was on the card one day. Hearing one of the bookies call: 'What price Cannabis?' he shouted: 'At Llanddewi Brefi, five pounds an ounce!'

Once, on a trip to the races he arrived carrying a bag. One of those travelling with him asked him whether he intended staying overnight. No, he didn't. But the bag was missing when he returned. That evening, before the crew headed for home, Smiles was involved in a card game in a pub and was doing well when he was accused of cheating. There were threats, but before it could come to blows a police inspector entered and cooled things down, buying a round for all those involved. He seemed eager not to see Smiles arrested.

Hughes' spending was legendary. He ordered a bespoke suit at B J Jones' clothes shop in Lampeter, worth around £300. He was measured, the suit duly made and Smiles was called down for a fitting. Pleased with the result, he handed the tailor a £100 tip.

Yes, in hindsight it should have been noticed that something very strange was going on. The Operation Julie police, of course, knew. Others, though they might have suspected, said nothing.

The sentencing did not signal the end of the story by any means. Two interesting events occurred in September 1979. Peter John Panting, a friend of Kemp and Bott who worked as a laboratory assistant at Tregaron Secondary School, had sued the publishers of Dick Lee's book, W H Allen and Co. for naming him as a member of the Angry Brigade. He was nothing of the sort. To complicate matters, a man who was a member of the Angry Brigade used Panting's identity. The real Panting was awarded a thousand pounds in compensation and an appropriate errata slip was placed in the remaining unsold copies.

The second incident involved the discovery of a cache of one million LSD tabs worth at least £5 million, not accounted for at the end of Operation Julie, buried in a wood near Ampthill, Bedfordshire. The discovery came about following a tip-off from a long-serving prisoner during the Operation Countryman inquiries into corruption among serving police officers from London and Bedfordshire. As a result of the operation, costing £2 million, it is believed that some 400 officers lost their jobs and it was recommended that 300 should face prosecution. A few did, but none were found guilty.

Many unanswered questions remain. If official

figures are correct in stating that the main producers and dealers made some £2 million a year, why was it that only £1 million was discovered? It is believed by some that Todd and Cuthbertson managed to hide around £2 million. In the case of Munro, no assets were discovered despite his long involvement in production.

In Hughes' case, there is a strong reason to believe that he received a tip-off regarding the impending raid. On the eve of the swoop he was drinking at the New Inn when he received a telephone call around midnight. Following the call, he left in a hurry. The following morning, despite a thorough search of the house and the garden being dug up, only £9,000 was found hidden in a cereal box and in a coin box connected to the telephone. Was this just a token sum left by Smiles? During the raid, a mystery girl was seen being escorted from his home by a Dyfed Powys police officer. She had been seen arriving the night before. Who was she? It is also alleged by some that Smiles was informed of the impending raid by a disgruntled Operation Julie officer. From the very beginning there has been talk of a royal connection. It is whispered that Princess Margaret was known to be involved with someone in the Cotswolds who was connected with one of the conspirators, and that the police deliberately postponed the raids until she was far enough away from the action.

In *Albion Dreaming*, Andy Roberts refers to a similar allegation. He alludes in particular to a story that appeared in the *News of the World* on 27 March 1977, the day after the raids. It reported: 'Seventy-one people were arrested. And a detective said last night that when the matter comes to court well-known names will be mentioned including a friend of the Royal Family.' Yet nothing more was heard of the story. But Roberts notes that there was a rumour circulating of one of those questioned selling 30,000 doses of LSD to someone acting on Margaret's behalf. I can confirm that I was given information implicating her and her 'friend' by a police officer. But was the dealer that supplied her 'friend' ever charged for that offence? No. The dealer's name was known to the police.

On the day after the principals were sentenced, Thursday, 9 March 1978, the *Express* led with a front-page story regarding a mysterious American, a new LSD Mr Big involved in negotiating the purchase of ergotamine tartrate in Switzerland. He had apparently bought 28 kilos, enough for someone like Richard Kemp to produce 20 pounds of pure acid, capable of yielding 110 million microdots. So much for ridding the world of up to 60 per cent of its LSD!

Sharing the front page was a picture story involving Princess Margaret holidaying on Mustique. She was shown enjoying herself on the beach while her current boyfriend, Roddy Llewellyn, was laid up in hospital suffering with internal bleeding. Was the proximity of the two stories mere coincidence or meant to convey a subliminal message? Was Lee still at it, exacting some kind of revenge through his favourite newspaper?

To return to Alston Hughes, it is a fact that the two undercover officers Wright and Bentley ingratiated themselves with him through, among other things,

selling him a wood-burning stove. To further confirm
their cover they told him that they had stolen it.
Hughes adapted it by removing its metal legs and
placing it on a specially-built stone plinth. On the
morning of the raid, the stove was burning. No-one
thought of moving it. There are some who believe
that Smiles' money and LSD stash were hidden in
the plinth. Shades of *The Great Escape*!

In essence, the story of Operation Julie was a clash,
not between the law and those who were breaking
it, but rather between two cultures – indeed two
worlds. In *Albion Dreaming*, Andy Roberts pinpoints
a definitive moment during Dennis Greenslade's
interrogation of Richard Kemp:

Kemp: You know nothing and you represent
political repression.

Greenslade: It's all very well to assume people have
a wonderful time on your LSD. We have to clean up
the mess. You have no appreciation of the amount
of people all over the country having personal
hallucinations.

Kemp: You know nothing.

Greenslade: I've travelled in the Far East and seen
people on opium.

Kemp: The opiates are something else. Acid is
different.

Greenslade: Whatever it is, it is against the law.

Kemp: The law, and you, represent political
repression.

There was obviously a total impasse. Andy
Roberts comments: 'This exchange demonstrated the

fundamental culture gap between the two sides. The police clearly knew little about what LSD was, what it did or how it was used by the counter culture. To them it was just another drug, albeit one that had more of a visible effect through its links to music, festivals, fashion and alternative life styles. Greenslade's attempt to sound knowledgeable by linking opium with LSD probably earned him Kemp's contempt, as the effects of the two drugs bear no relation to each other. Greenslade and his officers were rooted in the hard-core police drinking culture, and failed to understand LSD or its culture. Their ignorance must have come across strongly in the interviews with the Julie conspirators.'

And Roberts makes a valid point: 'The tenacity with which the police pursued the Operation Julie LSD conspiracy has rarely been equalled. It could be asked why, if the police, on a tight budget could smash the LSD ring, they could not do the same for the heroin trade. Heroin has killed more Britons every year than LSD has done since it was first synthesised.'

To Roberts, the conclusion is simple: 'The British establishment, that thousand-year-old interlocking web of legislated power, law, status and wealth seems unable to countenance anyone who wishes to expand their consciousness with LSD but is content to allow widespread abuse of heroin, barbiturates and alcohol.'

One fact that goes unmentioned in Dick Lee's book is that not one death could be directly attributed to Kemp's LSD. In his book, two girls who may have died from the consequences of taking acid are mentioned. However, no-one could prove the source of the acid involved. It is a known fact that the danger posed by LSD lies in its impurities. The purer the acid, the safer the dose. It therefore stands to reason that Kemp's almost 100-per-cent-pure acid was not only the purest but also the safest ever produced.

Was Operation Julie worth all the manpower and expense? Again there are conflicting views. LSD was illegal and the police smashed the biggest acid conspiracy in history. Martyn Pritchard alleged that smashing the two gangs led to such a scarcity of acid that its price jumped from around £1 to £8 a tab. This is totally contradicted, as we have seen, by the Release organisation. And at the Glastonbury Festival in 1981, acid was being sold for £1.50 a tab.

The free festivals, held mostly in the rural areas of south-west England and in mid and west Wales, were probably the closest manifestations of the mind revolution that LSD proponents campaigned for. As well as Windsor and Watchfield, there was the Stonehenge Festival. The most notable of those held in Wales was Meigan Fayre, the resurrection of an old hiring fair in the Preseli Mountains in Pembrokeshire, where the ancient blue stones of Stonehenge had been quarried. It was already the site of a hippy commune when the first fair of note was held in 1974. The fairs continued for the next two years. In 1975 it is estimated that the three-day festival attracted some 8,000 people. While there had been a scarcity of acid at Watchfield, Meigan

Fayre was awash with the stuff. Anyone experiencing a bad trip could rest and recover in a sanctuary tent. It remained empty, however. No bad trips were experienced there.

The free festivals continued well after the Julie trial. In 1979 the Psilocybin Fair was held in the Ystwyth Valley near Pontrhydygroes and the following year, the Festival of the New Hippies was held in the same location. The main drug here was the magic mushroom that grew wild in the area. Its possession was not illegal until it was reclassified as Class A in 2005. But LSD was also available. Seemingly respectable people from a wide area converged on the festival in the hope of catching a glimpse of naked hippies. They were not disappointed.

As for Operation Julie, there were no eventual winners. The psychedelic revolution ended – if it ever existed – not with a bang but a whimper. The Julie conspirators went down with hardly a word of protest from those who had been turned on by Kemp and Munro's acid. During the sentencing, one lone protester stood up in court and was quickly hustled out. The thousands who had thronged to the free festivals were notable by their absence as the conspirators were sentenced. Meanwhile, some of Kemp's LSD is still unearthed during occasional busts. It is as strong and pure today as when it was manufactured well over 30 years ago. Kemp himself had predicted that his acid would survive for a hundred years.

The police, who had worked diligently in almost impossible conditions, felt disillusioned and betrayed. Often they hit the brick wall of blind bureaucracy. Upon their return to normal duties, many were treated as if they had returned from a long holiday. They did not make the law; they merely swore to uphold it. Whatever the rights or wrongs of acid, they had performed well beyond the line of duty.

But did Dick Lee himself ultimately become a convert? Before tendering his resignation, he and his fellow officer Allen Buxton visited two LSD activists, Ronnie Laing and Steve Abrams. Laing was a psychiatrist and an acid user who had influenced Christine Bott, while Abrams was a parapsychologist who was also an acid advocate. Lee wanted to inform them that they had come close to being arrested because of their association with David Solomon. The meeting, according to what Abrams later disclosed to author David Black, led to a night of drinking and of arguing the pros and cons of LSD. Black states, 'Inspector Lee wanted Laing to explain how such intelligent men and women such as those he had just put behind bars could have become involved in the LSD trade.' Lee, says Black, was briefed on what Abrams and Laing saw 'as the unworkability of the Government's drug policy'. Lee and Buxton left during the early hours and both tendered their resignation a few hours later. Four others soon followed suit.

Operation Julie spawned hundreds of newspaper articles, various books, television documentaries and a three-part television drama starring Colin Blakely. A band named Drugs Squad released a song based on Operation Julie. As did The Remipeds and, in particular, The Clash with a song called 'Julie's Been Working for the Drug Squad' on their 1978 album,